45 Lemon Recipes for Home

By: Kelly Johnson

Table of Contents

- Classic Lemonade
- Lemon Butter Garlic Shrimp
- Lemon Blueberry Pancakes
- Lemon Herb Roast Chicken
- Lemon Garlic Butter Salmon
- Lemon Poppy Seed Muffins
- Lemon Basil Pesto Pasta
- Lemon Rosemary Roasted Potatoes
- Lemon Dill Greek Yogurt Sauce
- Lemon Garlic Hummus
- Lemon Butter Asparagus
- Lemon Ricotta Pancakes
- Lemon Garlic Butter Shrimp Scampi
- Lemon Raspberry Cheesecake
- Lemon Thyme Grilled Chicken
- Lemon Butter Garlic Knots
- Lemon Basil Grilled Corn
- Lemon Meringue Pie
- Lemon Garlic Butter Brussels Sprouts
- Lemon Herb Baked Cod
- Lemon Butter Chicken Piccata
- Lemon Coconut Energy Bites
- Lemon Basil Shrimp Pasta
- Lemon Garlic Butter Brussels Sprouts
- Lemon Raspberry Parfait
- Lemon Herb Baked Cod
- Lemon Butter Chicken Piccata
- Lemon Coconut Energy Bites
- Lemon Basil Shrimp Pasta
- Lemon Herb Quinoa Salad
- Lemon Garlic Butter Grilled Shrimp
- Lemon Almond Biscotti
- Lemon Ginger Chicken Stir-Fry
- Lemon Basil Vinaigrette
- Lemon Herb Couscous

- Lemon Garlic Butter Shrimp Tacos
- Lemon Raspberry Parfait
- Lemon Herb Chicken Skewers
- Lemon Butter Artichoke Dip
- Lemon Basil Pesto Hummus
- Lemon Garlic Butter Green Beans
- Lemon Berry Smoothie
- Lemon Sage Roasted CHicken
- Lemon Herb Quiche
- Lemon Butter Caper Pasta
- Lemon Rosemary Focaccia
- Lemon Garlic Butter Artichokes
- Lemon Basil Risotto
- Lemon Butter Garlic Shrimp Skewers
- Lemon Thyme Roasted Vegetables
- Lemon Cilantro Grilled Chicken

Classic Lemonade

Ingredients:

- 1 cup freshly squeezed lemon juice (about 4-6 lemons)
- 1 cup granulated sugar (adjust to taste)
- 5 cups cold water
- Ice cubes
- Lemon slices and mint leaves for garnish (optional)

Instructions:

Make Simple Syrup:
- In a small saucepan, combine 1 cup of water and the granulated sugar.
- Heat over medium heat, stirring occasionally until the sugar completely dissolves.
- Allow the simple syrup to cool. This will be your sweetener for the lemonade.

Juice the Lemons:
- Roll the lemons on a countertop to make them easier to juice.
- Cut the lemons in half and juice them using a citrus juicer or by hand.
- Strain the lemon juice to remove pulp and seeds, if desired.

Combine Ingredients:
- In a large pitcher, combine the freshly squeezed lemon juice with the simple syrup.
- Add 4 cups of cold water to the pitcher and stir well to mix.

Taste and Adjust:
- Taste the lemonade and adjust the sweetness by adding more sugar or water, if needed.

Chill:
- Refrigerate the lemonade for at least 1-2 hours to allow the flavors to meld and the mixture to chill.

Serve:
- Fill glasses with ice cubes and pour the chilled lemonade over the ice.
- Garnish with lemon slices and mint leaves if desired.

Enjoy:
- Stir the lemonade before serving, and enjoy your classic, homemade lemonade!

Feel free to customize this recipe by adding a splash of sparkling water for a fizzy version or experimenting with different herbs like basil or thyme for unique flavors. Adjust the sugar to your taste preference for the perfect balance of sweetness and tartness.

Lemon Butter Garlic Shrimp

Ingredients:

- 1 pound large shrimp, peeled and deveined
- 3 tablespoons unsalted butter
- 3 tablespoons olive oil
- 4 cloves garlic, minced
- 1 teaspoon red pepper flakes (optional, for some heat)
- 1/4 cup chicken or vegetable broth
- Juice of 1 lemon
- Zest of 1 lemon
- Salt and black pepper, to taste
- 2 tablespoons fresh parsley, chopped
- Lemon wedges for serving

Instructions:

Prepare the Shrimp:
- Pat the shrimp dry with paper towels and season them with salt and black pepper.

Sauté Shrimp:
- In a large skillet over medium-high heat, melt 2 tablespoons of butter with 2 tablespoons of olive oil.
- Add the shrimp to the skillet and cook for 2-3 minutes on each side until they turn pink and opaque. Remove the shrimp from the skillet and set aside.

Make the Garlic Butter Sauce:
- In the same skillet, add the remaining 1 tablespoon of butter and 1 tablespoon of olive oil.
- Add minced garlic and red pepper flakes (if using). Sauté for 1-2 minutes until the garlic becomes fragrant.

Deglaze with Broth:
- Pour in the chicken or vegetable broth, scraping any browned bits from the bottom of the skillet.

Add Lemon Juice and Zest:
- Stir in the lemon juice and lemon zest, allowing the flavors to meld for a minute.

Combine with Shrimp:

- Return the cooked shrimp to the skillet, tossing them in the garlic butter sauce to coat evenly.

Finish and Garnish:
- Season with additional salt and black pepper if needed. Sprinkle chopped fresh parsley over the shrimp.

Serve:
- Serve the lemon butter garlic shrimp over rice, pasta, or with crusty bread to soak up the flavorful sauce.
- Garnish with lemon wedges for an extra burst of citrus freshness.

This Lemon Butter Garlic Shrimp recipe delivers a perfect balance of rich, buttery, and zesty flavors. Enjoy this delicious dish as a quick and impressive meal for any occasion!

Lemon Blueberry Pancakes

Ingredients:

- 1 cup all-purpose flour
- 2 tablespoons granulated sugar
- 1 teaspoon baking powder
- 1/2 teaspoon baking soda
- 1/4 teaspoon salt
- 3/4 cup buttermilk
- 1 large egg
- 2 tablespoons unsalted butter, melted
- Zest of 1 lemon
- 1 tablespoon fresh lemon juice
- 1 cup fresh blueberries
- Butter or oil for cooking
- Maple syrup for serving
- Additional blueberries and lemon slices for garnish (optional)

Instructions:

Prepare Dry Ingredients:
- In a large bowl, whisk together the flour, sugar, baking powder, baking soda, and salt.

Mix Wet Ingredients:
- In a separate bowl, whisk together the buttermilk, egg, melted butter, lemon zest, and lemon juice.

Combine Wet and Dry Ingredients:
- Pour the wet ingredients into the dry ingredients and gently stir until just combined. Be careful not to overmix; it's okay if there are a few lumps.

Fold in Blueberries:
- Gently fold in the fresh blueberries into the pancake batter.

Preheat Griddle or Pan:
- Preheat a griddle or non-stick skillet over medium heat. Add a small amount of butter or oil to coat the surface.

Cook Pancakes:
- Pour 1/4 cup portions of batter onto the griddle for each pancake. Cook until bubbles form on the surface, then flip and cook until the other side is golden brown.

Keep Warm:
- Transfer cooked pancakes to a plate and keep warm. Repeat until all the batter is used.

Serve:
- Serve the lemon blueberry pancakes warm, drizzled with maple syrup.

Garnish (Optional):
- Garnish with additional blueberries and lemon slices if desired.

Enjoy:
- Enjoy these light and fluffy lemon blueberry pancakes for a delightful breakfast or brunch treat!

Feel free to customize these pancakes by adding a dollop of whipped cream or a sprinkle of powdered sugar for an extra touch of sweetness. The combination of zesty lemon and burst-in-your-mouth blueberries makes these pancakes a delicious and cheerful way to start your day.

Lemon Herb Roast Chicken

Ingredients:

- 1 whole chicken (about 4-5 pounds)
- Salt and black pepper, to taste
- 2 lemons, divided
- 4 cloves garlic, minced
- 2 tablespoons fresh rosemary, chopped
- 2 tablespoons fresh thyme, chopped
- 1/4 cup fresh parsley, chopped
- 1/4 cup olive oil
- 2 tablespoons unsalted butter, melted
- 1 cup chicken broth

Instructions:

Preheat Oven:
- Preheat the oven to 375°F (190°C).

Prepare Chicken:
- Pat the chicken dry with paper towels. Season the inside and outside of the chicken with salt and black pepper.

Zest and Juice Lemons:
- Zest one lemon and juice both lemons. Set aside.

Create Herb Rub:
- In a small bowl, combine the minced garlic, chopped rosemary, thyme, parsley, olive oil, melted butter, lemon zest, and half of the lemon juice. Mix well to create the herb rub.

Rub Chicken:
- Rub the herb mixture all over the chicken, making sure to get under the skin and inside the cavity.

Truss Chicken (Optional):
- Truss the chicken with kitchen twine if desired, to help it cook evenly.

Place in Roasting Pan:
- Place the seasoned chicken in a roasting pan, breast side up.

Roast:
- Roast the chicken in the preheated oven for about 1 to 1.5 hours, or until the internal temperature reaches 165°F (74°C) and the skin is golden brown and crispy.

Baste:
- Every 30 minutes, baste the chicken with the pan juices and the remaining lemon juice.

Rest:
- Once done, remove the chicken from the oven and let it rest for 10-15 minutes before carving.

Make Gravy (Optional):
- While the chicken is resting, you can make a simple gravy by deglazing the pan with chicken broth and reducing it on the stovetop. Strain if desired.

Serve:
- Carve the chicken and serve it with the optional gravy, garnishing with fresh herbs and lemon slices.

Enjoy the succulent and flavorful Lemon Herb Roast Chicken as the centerpiece of a delicious and comforting meal!

Lemon Garlic Butter Salmon

Ingredients:

- 4 salmon fillets (about 6 ounces each), skin-on
- Salt and black pepper, to taste
- 2 tablespoons olive oil
- 4 cloves garlic, minced
- 1/4 cup chicken or vegetable broth
- Juice of 1 lemon
- Zest of 1 lemon
- 2 tablespoons fresh parsley, chopped
- 4 tablespoons unsalted butter

Instructions:

Preheat Oven:
- Preheat the oven to 400°F (200°C).

Season Salmon:
- Pat the salmon fillets dry with paper towels. Season both sides with salt and black pepper.

Sear Salmon:
- In an oven-safe skillet, heat olive oil over medium-high heat. Place the salmon fillets in the skillet, skin-side down, and sear for 2-3 minutes until the skin is crispy.

Flip and Sauté:
- Flip the salmon fillets and sauté for an additional 1-2 minutes to sear the other side.

Prepare Lemon Garlic Butter:
- Push the salmon to the side of the skillet. Add minced garlic to the skillet and sauté for about 30 seconds until fragrant.

Deglaze with Broth:
- Pour in the chicken or vegetable broth to deglaze the skillet, scraping up any browned bits from the bottom.

Add Lemon Juice and Zest:
- Stir in the lemon juice and lemon zest, letting it simmer for 1-2 minutes.

Add Butter:
- Add the butter to the skillet, swirling it into the sauce until melted and well combined.

Baste Salmon:
- Spoon the lemon garlic butter sauce over the salmon fillets to coat them.

Bake:
- Transfer the skillet to the preheated oven and bake for 8-10 minutes or until the salmon is cooked to your liking.

Garnish:
- Remove from the oven and sprinkle chopped fresh parsley over the salmon.

Serve:
- Serve the Lemon Garlic Butter Salmon fillets with additional lemon slices on the side. Drizzle with extra sauce if desired.

Enjoy this elegant and flavorful Lemon Garlic Butter Salmon with its crispy skin, tender flesh, and the rich, citrusy butter sauce that perfectly complements the natural taste of the salmon.

Lemon Poppy Seed Muffins

Ingredients:

- 2 cups all-purpose flour
- 1 cup granulated sugar
- 1 tablespoon poppy seeds
- 1 tablespoon baking powder
- 1/2 teaspoon baking soda
- 1/4 teaspoon salt
- 1 cup plain yogurt or Greek yogurt
- 1/2 cup unsalted butter, melted and cooled
- 2 large eggs
- Zest of 2 lemons
- Juice of 1 lemon
- 1 teaspoon vanilla extract

For the Glaze:

- 1 cup confectioners' sugar
- 2-3 tablespoons fresh lemon juice

Instructions:

Preheat Oven:
- Preheat your oven to 375°F (190°C). Line a muffin tin with paper liners or grease the muffin cups.

Mix Dry Ingredients:
- In a large bowl, whisk together the flour, sugar, poppy seeds, baking powder, baking soda, and salt.

Combine Wet Ingredients:
- In another bowl, whisk together the yogurt, melted butter, eggs, lemon zest, lemon juice, and vanilla extract.

Combine Wet and Dry Ingredients:
- Pour the wet ingredients into the dry ingredients. Gently fold the mixture until just combined. Be careful not to overmix; it's okay if there are a few lumps.

Fill Muffin Cups:

- Spoon the batter into the prepared muffin cups, filling each about 2/3 full.

Bake:
- Bake in the preheated oven for 18-20 minutes or until a toothpick inserted into the center of a muffin comes out clean or with a few moist crumbs.

Cool:
- Allow the muffins to cool in the tin for 5 minutes, then transfer them to a wire rack to cool completely.

Prepare the Glaze:
- In a small bowl, whisk together confectioners' sugar and lemon juice until smooth. Adjust the consistency by adding more sugar or lemon juice if needed.

Glaze the Muffins:
- Drizzle the lemon glaze over the cooled muffins. Allow the glaze to set before serving.

Serve:
- Serve these delightful Lemon Poppy Seed Muffins with a cup of tea or coffee, and enjoy the burst of citrus flavor!

These muffins are a perfect balance of sweetness and tanginess, with the delightful crunch of poppy seeds. The glaze adds an extra layer of zesty goodness, making them a delicious treat for breakfast or anytime you crave a citrus-infused snack.

Lemon Basil Pesto Pasta

Ingredients:

For the Pesto:

- 2 cups fresh basil leaves, packed
- 1/2 cup grated Parmesan cheese
- 1/2 cup pine nuts or walnuts, toasted
- 3 cloves garlic, peeled
- Zest of 1 lemon
- Juice of 1 lemon
- 1/2 cup extra-virgin olive oil
- Salt and black pepper, to taste

For the Pasta:

- 12 ounces (about 350g) of your favorite pasta
- Salt for boiling water

Optional Garnishes:

- Extra Parmesan cheese
- Fresh basil leaves
- Cherry tomatoes, halved

Instructions:

Prepare Pesto:
- In a food processor, combine basil, Parmesan cheese, toasted nuts, garlic, lemon zest, and lemon juice. Pulse until coarsely chopped.

Stream in Olive Oil:
- With the food processor running, slowly stream in the olive oil until the pesto reaches a smooth and creamy consistency.

Season:
- Season the pesto with salt and black pepper to taste. Adjust the lemon juice or zest if desired.

Cook Pasta:
- Cook the pasta according to the package instructions in a large pot of salted boiling water until al dente.

Reserve Pasta Water:
- Before draining the pasta, reserve about 1/2 cup of pasta cooking water. This will help loosen the pesto and create a creamy sauce.

Combine Pasta and Pesto:
- Drain the cooked pasta and transfer it to a large mixing bowl. Add the prepared pesto and toss to coat the pasta evenly. If the pesto is too thick, add a bit of the reserved pasta water to achieve your desired consistency.

Garnish and Serve:
- Garnish the Lemon Basil Pesto Pasta with extra Parmesan cheese, fresh basil leaves, and halved cherry tomatoes if desired.

Serve Warm or Cold:
- Serve the pasta warm as a delightful main course or cold as a refreshing pasta salad.

Enjoy the vibrant and citrusy flavors of this Lemon Basil Pesto Pasta, a perfect dish for a quick and delicious meal. It's a celebration of fresh ingredients that come together to create a delightful burst of summer in every bite.

Lemon Rosemary Roasted Potatoes

Ingredients:

- 2 pounds (about 1 kg) baby potatoes, halved or quartered
- 3 tablespoons olive oil
- 2 tablespoons fresh rosemary, chopped
- Zest of 1 lemon
- Juice of 1 lemon
- 3 cloves garlic, minced
- Salt and black pepper, to taste
- Optional: Parmesan cheese, grated, for serving
- Fresh rosemary sprigs and lemon wedges for garnish

Instructions:

Preheat Oven:
- Preheat your oven to 400°F (200°C).

Prepare Potatoes:
- Wash and cut the baby potatoes into halves or quarters, depending on their size, for even roasting.

Make Marinade:
- In a large bowl, whisk together olive oil, chopped rosemary, lemon zest, lemon juice, minced garlic, salt, and black pepper.

Coat Potatoes:
- Add the halved or quartered potatoes to the bowl with the marinade. Toss until the potatoes are well coated with the mixture.

Roast Potatoes:
- Spread the potatoes evenly on a baking sheet in a single layer. Roast in the preheated oven for about 30-35 minutes or until the potatoes are golden brown and fork-tender. Turn the potatoes once or twice during roasting for even browning.

Optional Parmesan Topping:
- If desired, sprinkle grated Parmesan cheese over the potatoes during the last 10 minutes of roasting for a cheesy finish.

Garnish and Serve:
- Once the potatoes are done, remove them from the oven. Garnish with additional fresh rosemary sprigs and lemon wedges.

Serve Warm:
- Serve the Lemon Rosemary Roasted Potatoes warm as a delightful side dish.

Enjoy these aromatic and flavorful roasted potatoes with the earthy tones of rosemary and the zesty brightness of lemon. They make a perfect side dish for a variety of meals, from simple weeknight dinners to festive gatherings.

Lemon Dill Greek Yogurt Sauce

Ingredients:

- 1 cup Greek yogurt (full-fat or low-fat)
- 1 tablespoon fresh dill, finely chopped
- Zest of 1 lemon
- Juice of 1 lemon
- 1 clove garlic, minced
- 1 tablespoon extra-virgin olive oil
- Salt and black pepper, to taste

Instructions:

Prepare Greek Yogurt:
- In a bowl, combine the Greek yogurt, fresh dill, minced garlic, lemon zest, and lemon juice.

Mix Well:
- Stir the ingredients together until well combined.

Add Olive Oil:
- Drizzle in the extra-virgin olive oil and continue to stir until the sauce has a smooth and creamy consistency.

Season:
- Season the sauce with salt and black pepper to taste. Adjust the lemon juice or zest according to your preference.

Chill (Optional):
- For enhanced flavors, cover the bowl and let the sauce chill in the refrigerator for at least 30 minutes before serving.

Serve:
- Serve the Lemon Dill Greek Yogurt Sauce alongside grilled meats, fish, vegetables, or use it as a refreshing dip. It also makes a fantastic topping for salads or wraps.

Store:
- Store any leftover sauce in an airtight container in the refrigerator for up to 3-4 days.

This Lemon Dill Greek Yogurt Sauce is a versatile and light condiment that adds a burst of freshness to a variety of dishes. Whether you're looking for a dip, dressing, or topping, this sauce complements a wide range of meals with its zesty lemon and herby dill flavors.

Lemon Garlic Hummus

Ingredients:

- 1 can (15 ounces) chickpeas, drained and rinsed
- 3 tablespoons tahini (sesame paste)
- 2 cloves garlic, minced
- Zest of 1 lemon
- Juice of 1 lemon
- 1/4 cup extra-virgin olive oil, plus more for drizzling
- 1/2 teaspoon ground cumin
- Salt, to taste
- 2-3 tablespoons water (as needed for desired consistency)
- Optional: Paprika and fresh parsley for garnish

Instructions:

Prepare Chickpeas:
- Rinse and drain the canned chickpeas under cold water.

Peel Chickpeas (Optional):
- For an extra smooth texture, you can peel the skins off the chickpeas by gently pinching them. This step is optional but can result in a creamier hummus.

Combine Ingredients:
- In a food processor, combine chickpeas, tahini, minced garlic, lemon zest, lemon juice, olive oil, ground cumin, and a pinch of salt.

Blend:
- Process the ingredients until the mixture becomes smooth and creamy. If the hummus is too thick, add water gradually, blending until you reach your desired consistency.

Adjust Seasoning:
- Taste the hummus and adjust the seasoning by adding more salt or lemon juice as needed.

Serve:
- Transfer the Lemon Garlic Hummus to a serving bowl. Create a well in the center with the back of a spoon and drizzle with extra-virgin olive oil. Optionally, sprinkle with paprika and fresh parsley for garnish.

Chill (Optional):

- For enhanced flavors, cover the bowl and let the hummus chill in the refrigerator for at least 30 minutes before serving.

Enjoy:
- Serve the Lemon Garlic Hummus with pita bread, fresh veggies, or as a tasty spread for sandwiches and wraps.

This Lemon Garlic Hummus is a zesty and flavorful dip that is perfect for snacking or as a healthy appetizer. The combination of fresh lemon and garlic adds a vibrant kick to the classic hummus, making it a delightful addition to any gathering or meal.

Lemon Butter Asparagus

Ingredients:

- 1 bunch fresh asparagus spears, trimmed
- 2 tablespoons unsalted butter
- Zest of 1 lemon
- Juice of 1 lemon
- 2 cloves garlic, minced
- Salt and black pepper, to taste
- Optional: Grated Parmesan cheese for serving

Instructions:

Prepare Asparagus:
- Trim the tough ends from the asparagus spears. If desired, you can peel the lower part of the asparagus for a more tender texture.

Blanch Asparagus (Optional):
- In a large pot, bring water to a boil. Blanch the asparagus spears for 1-2 minutes, then immediately transfer them to a bowl of ice water to stop the cooking process. This step is optional and helps to preserve the vibrant green color.

Sauté Garlic:
- In a large skillet over medium heat, melt the butter. Add minced garlic and sauté for about 1 minute until fragrant.

Add Asparagus:
- Add the blanched or raw asparagus spears to the skillet. Toss them in the garlic butter to coat evenly.

Lemon Zest and Juice:
- Sprinkle the lemon zest over the asparagus and squeeze the lemon juice. Toss to combine.

Sauté Until Tender:
- Continue to cook the asparagus for 3-5 minutes or until they are crisp-tender. Be careful not to overcook; you want them to be vibrant and slightly crunchy.

Season:
- Season the asparagus with salt and black pepper to taste. Adjust the seasoning if needed.

Serve:
- Transfer the Lemon Butter Asparagus to a serving platter. Optionally, sprinkle with grated Parmesan cheese before serving.

Enjoy:
- Serve this vibrant and flavorful side dish alongside your favorite main course. It's a perfect complement to chicken, fish, or any meal that could use a burst of lemony freshness.

This Lemon Butter Asparagus recipe is a quick and elegant way to prepare this delicious and nutritious vegetable. The combination of zesty lemon, garlic, and butter enhances the natural flavors of the asparagus, creating a delightful side dish that's perfect for any occasion.

Lemon Ricotta Pancakes

Ingredients:

- 1 cup all-purpose flour
- 1 tablespoon sugar
- 1 teaspoon baking powder
- 1/2 teaspoon baking soda
- 1/4 teaspoon salt
- 1 cup ricotta cheese
- 2/3 cup milk
- 2 large eggs
- Zest of 2 lemons
- Juice of 1 lemon
- Butter or oil for cooking
- Optional toppings: Fresh berries, maple syrup, powdered sugar

Instructions:

Preheat Griddle or Pan:
- Preheat a griddle or non-stick skillet over medium heat.

Mix Dry Ingredients:
- In a large bowl, whisk together the flour, sugar, baking powder, baking soda, and salt.

Prepare Wet Ingredients:
- In a separate bowl, combine the ricotta cheese, milk, eggs, lemon zest, and lemon juice. Mix well until smooth.

Combine Wet and Dry Ingredients:
- Pour the wet ingredients into the dry ingredients and stir until just combined. The batter may be slightly lumpy.

Cook Pancakes:
- Grease the griddle or skillet with butter or oil. Pour 1/4 cup portions of batter onto the hot surface, spreading it slightly with the back of a spoon.

Flip and Cook:
- Cook until bubbles form on the surface of the pancakes and the edges look set. Flip and cook the other side until golden brown.

Repeat:
- Repeat with the remaining batter, adding more butter or oil to the griddle as needed.

Serve:
- Serve the Lemon Ricotta Pancakes warm with your favorite toppings. Fresh berries, maple syrup, and a sprinkle of powdered sugar work well.

Enjoy:
- Enjoy these light and fluffy pancakes that are infused with the delightful flavors of lemon and ricotta.

These Lemon Ricotta Pancakes are a delightful twist on the classic breakfast favorite. The ricotta adds a creamy texture, while the lemon provides a refreshing citrusy zing. Perfect for a leisurely brunch or a special breakfast treat!

Lemon Garlic Butter Shrimp Scampi

Ingredients:

- 1 pound large shrimp, peeled and deveined
- Salt and black pepper, to taste
- 8 ounces linguine or spaghetti
- 3 tablespoons unsalted butter
- 3 tablespoons olive oil
- 4 cloves garlic, minced
- 1/2 teaspoon red pepper flakes (adjust to taste)
- Zest of 1 lemon
- Juice of 1 lemon
- 1/2 cup dry white wine (optional)
- 1/4 cup chicken broth
- 1/4 cup fresh parsley, chopped
- Grated Parmesan cheese for serving (optional)

Instructions:

Prepare Shrimp:
- Pat the shrimp dry with paper towels and season with salt and black pepper.

Cook Pasta:
- Cook the linguine or spaghetti according to the package instructions in a large pot of salted boiling water. Drain and set aside.

Sauté Shrimp:
- In a large skillet, heat 2 tablespoons of butter and 2 tablespoons of olive oil over medium-high heat. Add the seasoned shrimp to the skillet and cook for 2-3 minutes on each side until they turn pink and opaque. Remove the shrimp from the skillet and set aside.

Make Lemon Garlic Sauce:
- In the same skillet, add the remaining 1 tablespoon of butter and 1 tablespoon of olive oil. Add minced garlic and red pepper flakes, sauté for about 1 minute until fragrant.

Deglaze with Wine (Optional):
- If using white wine, pour it into the skillet to deglaze, scraping up any browned bits from the bottom.

Add Lemon Zest and Juice:

- Stir in the lemon zest and lemon juice, allowing the flavors to meld for a minute.

Combine with Shrimp:
- Return the cooked shrimp to the skillet, tossing them in the lemon garlic sauce.

Add Chicken Broth:
- Pour in the chicken broth, allowing the sauce to simmer for 2-3 minutes.

Combine with Pasta:
- Add the cooked pasta to the skillet, tossing to coat the pasta evenly with the lemon garlic butter sauce.

Finish and Garnish:
- Sprinkle chopped fresh parsley over the shrimp scampi and pasta.

Serve:
- Serve the Lemon Garlic Butter Shrimp Scampi warm, optionally garnished with grated Parmesan cheese.

Enjoy this delightful Lemon Garlic Butter Shrimp Scampi, a restaurant-quality dish that comes together quickly and is bursting with vibrant flavors. Perfect for a quick weeknight dinner or a special occasion.

Lemon Raspberry Cheesecake

Ingredients:

For the Crust:

- 1 1/2 cups graham cracker crumbs
- 1/3 cup unsalted butter, melted
- 2 tablespoons granulated sugar

For the Cheesecake Filling:

- 4 packages (8 ounces each) cream cheese, softened
- 1 cup granulated sugar
- 4 large eggs
- 1/2 cup sour cream
- 1/2 cup fresh lemon juice
- Zest of 2 lemons
- 1 teaspoon vanilla extract

For the Raspberry Swirl:

- 1 cup fresh raspberries
- 2 tablespoons granulated sugar
- 1 tablespoon water

For Topping (Optional):

- Fresh raspberries
- Lemon zest
- Whipped cream

Instructions:

Preheat Oven:
- Preheat your oven to 325°F (163°C). Grease a 9-inch springform pan.

Make the Crust:

- In a bowl, combine the graham cracker crumbs, melted butter, and sugar. Press the mixture into the bottom of the prepared springform pan. Use the back of a spoon to create an even crust.

Bake Crust:
- Bake the crust in the preheated oven for 10 minutes. Remove and let it cool while you prepare the filling.

Prepare Raspberry Swirl:
- In a small saucepan, combine the raspberries, sugar, and water over medium heat. Cook for 5-7 minutes, mashing the raspberries with a fork. Strain the mixture to remove seeds, leaving you with a smooth raspberry sauce.

Make the Cheesecake Filling:
- In a large bowl, beat the cream cheese until smooth using an electric mixer. Add the sugar and continue to beat until well combined.
- Add the eggs one at a time, beating well after each addition.
- Mix in the sour cream, lemon juice, lemon zest, and vanilla extract until the batter is smooth and creamy.

Pour Batter into Crust:
- Pour the cheesecake batter over the cooled crust in the springform pan.

Add Raspberry Swirl:
- Spoon dollops of the raspberry sauce onto the cheesecake batter. Use a knife or toothpick to create a swirl pattern.

Bake Cheesecake:
- Bake the cheesecake in the preheated oven for 50-60 minutes, or until the center is set and the edges are slightly golden.

Cool and Refrigerate:
- Allow the cheesecake to cool in the pan, then refrigerate for at least 4 hours or overnight.

Decorate and Serve:
- Before serving, top the cheesecake with fresh raspberries, lemon zest, and a dollop of whipped cream if desired.

Enjoy:
- Slice and enjoy the luscious combination of lemon and raspberry in this delightful cheesecake!

This Lemon Raspberry Cheesecake is a perfect blend of creamy richness and fruity brightness, making it an elegant dessert for any special occasion.

Lemon Thyme Grilled Chicken

Ingredients:

- 4 boneless, skinless chicken breasts
- 1/4 cup olive oil
- Zest of 1 lemon
- Juice of 2 lemons
- 3 cloves garlic, minced
- 1 tablespoon fresh thyme leaves, chopped
- 1 teaspoon honey
- Salt and black pepper, to taste
- Lemon slices and fresh thyme sprigs for garnish

Instructions:

Prepare Marinade:
- In a bowl, whisk together olive oil, lemon zest, lemon juice, minced garlic, chopped thyme, honey, salt, and black pepper.

Marinate Chicken:
- Place the chicken breasts in a shallow dish or a resealable plastic bag. Pour the marinade over the chicken, making sure each piece is well coated. Marinate in the refrigerator for at least 30 minutes, or up to 4 hours for optimal flavor.

Preheat Grill:
- Preheat your grill to medium-high heat.

Grill Chicken:
- Remove the chicken from the marinade and shake off excess. Grill the chicken breasts for about 6-8 minutes per side or until they reach an internal temperature of 165°F (74°C) and the juices run clear.

Baste with Marinade (Optional):
- Optionally, you can baste the chicken with some of the marinade during the grilling process for additional flavor.

Rest:
- Once done, transfer the grilled chicken to a plate and let it rest for a few minutes.

Garnish:
- Garnish the Lemon Thyme Grilled Chicken with lemon slices and fresh thyme sprigs.

Serve:
- Serve the grilled chicken with your favorite sides, such as roasted vegetables, a fresh salad, or rice.

Enjoy the succulent and aromatic flavors of this Lemon Thyme Grilled Chicken. The combination of citrusy lemon and earthy thyme creates a delightful dish that's perfect for a summertime barbecue or any outdoor gathering.

Lemon Butter Garlic Knots

Ingredients:

For the Dough:

- 1 pound pizza dough (store-bought or homemade)
- Flour for dusting

For the Lemon Butter Garlic Sauce:

- 1/2 cup unsalted butter
- 4 cloves garlic, minced
- Zest of 1 lemon
- Juice of 1 lemon
- 2 tablespoons fresh parsley, chopped
- Salt, to taste

For Finishing:

- Grated Parmesan cheese
- Additional chopped parsley for garnish

Instructions:

Preheat Oven:
- Preheat your oven according to the pizza dough package instructions or recipe.

Prepare Dough:
- On a floured surface, roll out the pizza dough into a large rectangle.

Cut Dough Strips:
- Cut the rolled-out dough into strips, about 1.5 inches wide and 6-8 inches long.

Tie into Knots:
- Take each strip and tie it into a knot, placing the ends underneath. Arrange the knots on a baking sheet lined with parchment paper.

Bake Dough:
- Bake the knots in the preheated oven according to the pizza dough package instructions or recipe until they are golden brown and cooked through.

Make Lemon Butter Garlic Sauce:
- While the knots are baking, prepare the lemon butter garlic sauce. In a small saucepan, melt the butter over medium heat. Add minced garlic and sauté until fragrant.

Add Lemon Zest and Juice:
- Stir in the lemon zest and lemon juice. Allow the mixture to simmer for a couple of minutes.

Season and Add Parsley:
- Season the sauce with salt to taste. Stir in chopped fresh parsley and remove the saucepan from heat.

Coat Knots:
- Once the knots are out of the oven, brush them generously with the lemon butter garlic sauce while they are still warm.

Finish and Garnish:
- Sprinkle grated Parmesan cheese over the knots and garnish with additional chopped parsley.

Serve:
- Serve the Lemon Butter Garlic Knots warm as a delightful appetizer or side dish.

These Lemon Butter Garlic Knots are a flavorful twist on the classic garlic knots. The combination of zesty lemon, rich butter, and garlic creates a mouthwatering experience. Perfect for serving with pasta, soups, or as a delicious snack!

Lemon Basil Grilled Corn

Ingredients:

- 4 ears of fresh corn, husks removed
- 1/4 cup unsalted butter, melted
- Zest of 1 lemon
- Juice of 1 lemon
- 2 tablespoons fresh basil, chopped
- Salt and black pepper, to taste
- Grated Parmesan cheese (optional, for serving)

Instructions:

Preheat Grill:
- Preheat your grill to medium-high heat.

Prepare Corn:
- Husk the corn and remove the silk. Rinse the corn under cold water.

Grill Corn:
- Place the corn directly on the preheated grill. Grill for about 10-15 minutes, turning occasionally, until the corn is cooked and has a nice char.

Prepare Lemon Basil Butter:
- In a small bowl, mix melted butter with lemon zest, lemon juice, and chopped fresh basil.

Brush Corn with Lemon Basil Butter:
- Once the corn is done grilling, brush each ear with the lemon basil butter mixture, ensuring they are evenly coated.

Season:
- Sprinkle salt and black pepper over the grilled corn to taste. Adjust the seasoning if needed.

Optional: Parmesan Cheese:
- Optionally, sprinkle grated Parmesan cheese over the corn while the butter is still warm.

Serve:
- Serve the Lemon Basil Grilled Corn immediately, either whole or sliced into smaller pieces.

Enjoy this flavorful and aromatic twist on classic grilled corn. The combination of zesty lemon and fragrant basil adds a delightful freshness to the smoky, charred corn. Perfect as a side dish for summer barbecues or outdoor gatherings.

Lemon Meringue Pie

Ingredients:

For the Pie Crust:

- 1 1/4 cups all-purpose flour
- 1/2 cup unsalted butter, cold and cubed
- 1/4 cup granulated sugar
- 1/4 teaspoon salt
- 3-4 tablespoons ice water

For the Lemon Filling:

- 1 cup granulated sugar
- 3 tablespoons cornstarch
- 1/4 teaspoon salt
- 1 1/2 cups water
- 4 large egg yolks, beaten
- 1 tablespoon lemon zest
- 1/2 cup fresh lemon juice
- 2 tablespoons unsalted butter

For the Meringue:

- 4 large egg whites, at room temperature
- 1/4 teaspoon cream of tartar
- 1/2 cup granulated sugar
- 1/2 teaspoon vanilla extract

Instructions:

Prepare Pie Crust:

In a food processor, combine the flour, sugar, and salt. Add the cold, cubed butter and pulse until the mixture resembles coarse crumbs.
Gradually add ice water, one tablespoon at a time, pulsing until the dough comes together. Form the dough into a disc, wrap it in plastic wrap, and refrigerate for at least 1 hour.

Preheat the oven to 375°F (190°C). Roll out the chilled dough on a floured surface and fit it into a 9-inch pie dish. Trim and crimp the edges. Prick the bottom with a fork and line with parchment paper and pie weights or dried beans.

Bake the crust for about 15 minutes, then remove the weights and parchment paper and bake for an additional 10-15 minutes or until golden brown. Allow the crust to cool completely.

Prepare Lemon Filling:

In a medium saucepan, whisk together sugar, cornstarch, and salt. Gradually whisk in water until smooth. Bring the mixture to a boil over medium heat, stirring constantly.

In a separate bowl, whisk the beaten egg yolks. Gradually whisk in about 1 cup of the hot sugar mixture to temper the eggs. Pour the tempered eggs back into the saucepan, whisking constantly.

Cook the mixture over medium heat, stirring constantly, until it thickens. Remove from heat and stir in lemon zest, lemon juice, and butter. Allow the filling to cool slightly.

Pour the lemon filling into the cooled pie crust. Cover the surface with plastic wrap to prevent a skin from forming, and refrigerate while preparing the meringue.

Prepare Meringue:

Preheat the oven to 325°F (163°C).

In a clean, dry bowl, beat the egg whites with cream of tartar until soft peaks form. Gradually add sugar, one tablespoon at a time, and continue beating until stiff, glossy peaks form. Beat in vanilla extract.

Assemble and Bake:

Remove the plastic wrap from the lemon filling. Spoon the meringue over the lemon filling, spreading it to the edges to seal the pie.

Use the back of a spoon to create peaks in the meringue.

Bake in the preheated oven for about 15-20 minutes or until the meringue is golden brown.

Allow the pie to cool to room temperature, then refrigerate for at least 2 hours before serving.

Slice and enjoy your delicious Lemon Meringue Pie!

This classic Lemon Meringue Pie combines a buttery crust, tangy lemon filling, and a fluffy meringue topping for a delightful and refreshing dessert.

Lemon Garlic Butter Brussels Sprouts

Ingredients:

- 1 pound Brussels sprouts, trimmed and halved
- 2 tablespoons unsalted butter
- 2 tablespoons olive oil
- 4 cloves garlic, minced
- Zest of 1 lemon
- Juice of 1 lemon
- Salt and black pepper, to taste
- Grated Parmesan cheese (optional, for serving)
- Chopped fresh parsley (optional, for garnish)

Instructions:

Preheat Oven:
- Preheat your oven to 400°F (200°C).

Prepare Brussels Sprouts:
- Trim the ends of the Brussels sprouts and cut them in half. Remove any outer leaves that appear yellow or damaged.

Roast Brussels Sprouts:
- Place the halved Brussels sprouts on a baking sheet. Drizzle with olive oil, sprinkle with salt and black pepper, and toss to coat evenly. Roast in the preheated oven for 20-25 minutes or until the Brussels sprouts are golden brown and crispy on the edges.

Make Lemon Garlic Butter:
- In a small saucepan, melt the butter over medium heat. Add minced garlic and sauté for 1-2 minutes until fragrant.

Add Lemon Zest and Juice:
- Stir in the lemon zest and lemon juice, allowing the flavors to meld for another minute.

Combine with Brussels Sprouts:
- Once the Brussels sprouts are done roasting, transfer them to a large bowl. Pour the lemon garlic butter over the Brussels sprouts and toss to coat evenly.

Adjust Seasoning:
- Taste and adjust the seasoning with salt and black pepper if needed.

Optional: Parmesan Cheese:

- Optionally, sprinkle grated Parmesan cheese over the Brussels sprouts while they are still warm.

Garnish:
- Garnish with chopped fresh parsley for a burst of color and freshness.

Serve:
- Serve the Lemon Garlic Butter Brussels Sprouts warm as a flavorful and vibrant side dish.

These Lemon Garlic Butter Brussels Sprouts are a tasty and elegant way to enjoy this nutritious vegetable. The combination of zesty lemon and savory garlic butter enhances the natural flavors of the Brussels sprouts, making them a perfect accompaniment to any meal.

Lemon Herb Baked Cod

Ingredients:

- 4 cod fillets (about 6 ounces each)
- 3 tablespoons olive oil
- 2 tablespoons fresh lemon juice
- 1 tablespoon fresh parsley, chopped
- 1 teaspoon fresh thyme leaves
- 1 teaspoon fresh rosemary, chopped
- 2 cloves garlic, minced
- Zest of 1 lemon
- Salt and black pepper, to taste
- Lemon slices (for garnish)
- Fresh herbs (for garnish)

Instructions:

Preheat Oven:
- Preheat your oven to 400°F (200°C).

Prepare Cod Fillets:
- Pat the cod fillets dry with paper towels and place them in a baking dish.

Make Lemon Herb Marinade:
- In a small bowl, whisk together olive oil, lemon juice, chopped parsley, thyme, rosemary, minced garlic, and lemon zest.

Marinate Cod:
- Pour the lemon herb marinade over the cod fillets, ensuring they are evenly coated. Allow them to marinate for about 15-20 minutes.

Season:
- Season the cod fillets with salt and black pepper to taste.

Bake Cod:
- Bake the cod in the preheated oven for 15-20 minutes or until the fish is opaque and easily flakes with a fork.

Optional Broil:
- For a golden finish, you can broil the cod for an additional 1-2 minutes after baking.

Garnish:
- Garnish the Lemon Herb Baked Cod with lemon slices and fresh herbs.

Serve:

- Serve the cod fillets warm with your favorite side dishes, such as steamed vegetables or rice.

This Lemon Herb Baked Cod is a light and flavorful dish that celebrates the natural taste of the fish. The combination of fresh herbs and zesty lemon creates a vibrant and aromatic meal. Perfect for a quick and healthy dinner option.

Lemon Butter Chicken Piccata

Ingredients:

- 4 boneless, skinless chicken breasts
- Salt and black pepper, to taste
- 1 cup all-purpose flour, for dredging
- 4 tablespoons unsalted butter, divided
- 2 tablespoons olive oil
- 1/2 cup chicken broth
- 1/2 cup dry white wine
- Juice of 2 lemons
- 1/4 cup capers, drained
- 1/4 cup fresh parsley, chopped
- Lemon slices, for garnish

Instructions:

Prep Chicken:
- Season the chicken breasts with salt and black pepper.

Dredge in Flour:
- Dredge each chicken breast in flour, shaking off any excess.

Sear Chicken:
- In a large skillet, heat 2 tablespoons of butter and olive oil over medium-high heat. Add the chicken breasts and cook for about 4-5 minutes per side or until golden brown and cooked through. Transfer the cooked chicken to a plate and cover with foil to keep warm.

Make Sauce:
- In the same skillet, add the chicken broth, white wine, and lemon juice. Use a wooden spoon to scrape up any browned bits from the bottom of the pan.

Add Capers and Parsley:
- Stir in the capers and chopped parsley. Let the sauce simmer for 2-3 minutes to reduce slightly.

Finish with Butter:
- Reduce the heat to low, and whisk in the remaining 2 tablespoons of butter until the sauce is smooth and slightly thickened.

Return Chicken to Pan:

- Return the cooked chicken breasts to the skillet, coating them with the lemon butter sauce. Cook for an additional 2-3 minutes to heat through.

Garnish:
- Garnish the Lemon Butter Chicken Piccata with lemon slices and additional chopped parsley.

Serve:
- Serve the chicken over pasta, rice, or with your favorite side dishes. Spoon the lemon butter caper sauce over the chicken.

Enjoy this classic and flavorful Lemon Butter Chicken Piccata, featuring tender chicken breasts in a tangy and buttery lemon caper sauce. It's a delicious and elegant dish that's perfect for a special dinner.

Lemon Coconut Energy Bites

Ingredients:

- 1 cup Medjool dates, pitted
- 1 cup unsweetened shredded coconut
- 1/2 cup raw cashews
- Zest of 2 lemons
- Juice of 1 lemon
- 1 tablespoon chia seeds
- 1/2 teaspoon vanilla extract
- Pinch of salt (optional)
- Additional shredded coconut for rolling (optional)

Instructions:

Prepare Dates:
- If the dates are not soft, soak them in warm water for about 10 minutes. Drain well.

Combine Ingredients:
- In a food processor, combine dates, shredded coconut, raw cashews, lemon zest, lemon juice, chia seeds, vanilla extract, and a pinch of salt if desired.

Process Mixture:
- Process the mixture until it comes together into a sticky, crumbly dough. You should be able to pinch the mixture between your fingers, and it holds together.

Form Energy Bites:
- Take small portions of the mixture and roll them between your palms to form bite-sized energy balls. If the mixture is too sticky, you can wet your hands or dust them with additional shredded coconut.

Optional: Roll in Coconut:
- Optionally, roll the energy bites in additional shredded coconut for a coating.

Chill:
- Place the energy bites in the refrigerator for at least 30 minutes to firm up.

Store:

- Store the Lemon Coconut Energy Bites in an airtight container in the refrigerator for freshness.

Enjoy:
- Enjoy these refreshing and nutritious energy bites as a quick and healthy snack.

These Lemon Coconut Energy Bites are a delightful combination of sweet and tangy flavors, providing a burst of energy and satisfaction. Packed with wholesome ingredients, they make for a convenient and delicious on-the-go snack.

Lemon Basil Shrimp Pasta

Ingredients:

- 8 ounces linguine or your choice of pasta
- 1 pound large shrimp, peeled and deveined
- Salt and black pepper, to taste
- 3 tablespoons olive oil
- 4 cloves garlic, minced
- Zest of 1 lemon
- Juice of 1 lemon
- 1/2 cup cherry tomatoes, halved
- 1/4 cup fresh basil, chopped
- 1/4 cup freshly grated Parmesan cheese (optional)
- Red pepper flakes (optional, for heat)

Instructions:

Cook Pasta:
- Cook the pasta according to package instructions in a large pot of salted boiling water. Drain and set aside.

Season Shrimp:
- Season the shrimp with salt and black pepper.

Sauté Shrimp:
- In a large skillet, heat olive oil over medium-high heat. Add the seasoned shrimp and cook for 2-3 minutes per side or until they turn pink and opaque. Remove the shrimp from the skillet and set aside.

Make Lemon Garlic Sauce:
- In the same skillet, add minced garlic and sauté for about 1 minute until fragrant. Add the lemon zest and lemon juice, stirring to combine.

Combine Pasta and Shrimp:
- Return the cooked pasta to the skillet, tossing it in the lemon garlic sauce. Add the cooked shrimp back to the skillet.

Add Tomatoes and Basil:
- Add halved cherry tomatoes and chopped fresh basil to the pasta and shrimp. Toss everything together until well combined.

Optional: Add Parmesan and Red Pepper Flakes:
- If desired, sprinkle freshly grated Parmesan cheese over the pasta and shrimp. Add red pepper flakes for a bit of heat.

Serve:
- Serve the Lemon Basil Shrimp Pasta warm, garnished with additional fresh basil and a wedge of lemon if desired.

This Lemon Basil Shrimp Pasta is a light and flavorful dish that combines the freshness of lemon and basil with succulent shrimp. It's quick to make and perfect for a satisfying weeknight dinner.

Lemon Garlic Butter Brussels Sprouts

Ingredients:

- 1 pound Brussels sprouts, trimmed and halved
- 3 tablespoons unsalted butter
- 3 tablespoons olive oil
- 4 cloves garlic, minced
- Zest of 1 lemon
- Juice of 1 lemon
- Salt and black pepper, to taste
- Grated Parmesan cheese (optional, for serving)
- Fresh parsley, chopped (optional, for garnish)

Instructions:

Preheat Oven:
- Preheat your oven to 400°F (200°C).

Prepare Brussels Sprouts:
- Trim the ends of the Brussels sprouts and cut them in half. Remove any outer leaves that appear yellow or damaged.

Roast Brussels Sprouts:
- Place the halved Brussels sprouts on a baking sheet. Drizzle with olive oil, sprinkle with salt and black pepper, and toss to coat evenly. Roast in the preheated oven for 20-25 minutes or until the Brussels sprouts are golden brown and crispy on the edges.

Make Lemon Garlic Butter:
- In a small saucepan, melt the butter over medium heat. Add minced garlic and sauté for 1-2 minutes until fragrant.

Add Lemon Zest and Juice:
- Stir in the lemon zest and lemon juice. Allow the mixture to simmer for a couple of minutes.

Combine with Brussels Sprouts:
- Once the Brussels sprouts are done roasting, transfer them to a large bowl. Pour the lemon garlic butter over the Brussels sprouts and toss to coat evenly.

Adjust Seasoning:
- Taste and adjust the seasoning with salt and black pepper if needed.

Optional: Parmesan Cheese:
- Optionally, sprinkle grated Parmesan cheese over the Brussels sprouts while they are still warm.

Garnish:
- Garnish with chopped fresh parsley for a burst of color and freshness.

Serve:
- Serve the Lemon Garlic Butter Brussels Sprouts warm as a flavorful and vibrant side dish.

These Lemon Garlic Butter Brussels Sprouts are a delightful combination of zesty lemon, savory garlic butter, and perfectly roasted Brussels sprouts. They make a fantastic side dish for any meal and are sure to be a hit at your dinner table.

Lemon Raspberry Parfait

Ingredients:

For the Lemon Cream:

- 1 cup heavy cream
- 1/4 cup powdered sugar
- 1 teaspoon vanilla extract
- Zest of 1 lemon
- 2 tablespoons fresh lemon juice

For the Raspberry Sauce:

- 1 cup fresh raspberries
- 2 tablespoons granulated sugar
- 1 tablespoon water

For Assembly:

- Lemon cream
- Raspberry sauce
- Greek yogurt or vanilla yogurt
- Granola
- Fresh raspberries
- Lemon slices (for garnish)
- Mint leaves (for garnish, optional)

Instructions:

Prepare Lemon Cream:

In a chilled mixing bowl, whip the heavy cream until soft peaks form.
Add powdered sugar, vanilla extract, lemon zest, and lemon juice to the whipped cream. Continue whipping until stiff peaks form.

Prepare Raspberry Sauce:

In a small saucepan, combine fresh raspberries, granulated sugar, and water. Cook over medium heat, stirring occasionally, until the raspberries break down and the mixture thickens to a sauce-like consistency. Remove from heat and let it cool.

Assemble the Parfait:

In serving glasses or jars, layer the components as follows:
- Start with a spoonful of lemon cream at the bottom.
- Add a layer of Greek yogurt or vanilla yogurt.
- Drizzle a spoonful of raspberry sauce over the yogurt.
- Sprinkle granola over the sauce for added crunch.
- Repeat the layers until you reach the top of the glass, finishing with a dollop of lemon cream.

Top each parfait with fresh raspberries, lemon slices, and mint leaves for a decorative touch.
Chill the parfaits in the refrigerator for at least 30 minutes before serving.
Serve chilled and enjoy your delightful Lemon Raspberry Parfait!

This Lemon Raspberry Parfait is a refreshing and visually appealing dessert that combines the tartness of raspberries with the bright citrus flavor of lemon. It's perfect for a light and elegant treat, especially during warmer seasons.

Lemon Herb Baked Cod

Ingredients:

- 4 cod fillets (about 6 ounces each)
- Salt and black pepper, to taste
- 3 tablespoons olive oil
- 2 tablespoons fresh lemon juice
- 1 tablespoon fresh parsley, chopped
- 1 teaspoon fresh thyme leaves
- 1 teaspoon fresh rosemary, chopped
- 2 cloves garlic, minced
- Zest of 1 lemon
- Lemon slices (for garnish)

Instructions:

Preheat Oven:
- Preheat your oven to 400°F (200°C).

Season Cod Fillets:
- Pat the cod fillets dry with paper towels. Season both sides with salt and black pepper.

Prepare Lemon Herb Marinade:
- In a small bowl, whisk together olive oil, fresh lemon juice, chopped parsley, thyme leaves, rosemary, minced garlic, and lemon zest.

Marinate Cod:
- Place the cod fillets in a baking dish. Pour the lemon herb marinade over the fillets, making sure they are well coated. Allow them to marinate for about 15 minutes.

Bake Cod:
- Bake the cod in the preheated oven for 15-20 minutes or until the fish is opaque and easily flakes with a fork.

Optional Broil:
- For a golden finish, you can broil the cod for an additional 1-2 minutes after baking.

Garnish:
- Garnish the Lemon Herb Baked Cod with lemon slices.

Serve:

- Serve the cod fillets warm with your favorite side dishes, such as steamed vegetables, quinoa, or a fresh salad.

This Lemon Herb Baked Cod is a light and flavorful dish that's easy to prepare. The combination of fresh herbs and zesty lemon adds a delightful touch to the mild flavor of cod. It's a perfect choice for a quick and healthy dinner option.

Lemon Butter Chicken Piccata

Ingredients:

- 4 boneless, skinless chicken breasts
- Salt and black pepper, to taste
- 1 cup all-purpose flour, for dredging
- 4 tablespoons unsalted butter, divided
- 2 tablespoons olive oil
- 1/2 cup chicken broth
- 1/2 cup dry white wine
- Juice of 2 lemons
- 1/4 cup capers, drained
- 1/4 cup fresh parsley, chopped
- Lemon slices (for garnish)

Instructions:

Prep Chicken:
- Season the chicken breasts with salt and black pepper.

Dredge in Flour:
- Dredge each chicken breast in flour, shaking off any excess.

Sear Chicken:
- In a large skillet, heat 2 tablespoons of butter and olive oil over medium-high heat. Add the chicken breasts and cook for about 4-5 minutes per side or until golden brown and cooked through. Transfer the cooked chicken to a plate and cover with foil to keep warm.

Make Sauce:
- In the same skillet, add the chicken broth, white wine, and lemon juice. Use a wooden spoon to scrape up any browned bits from the bottom of the pan.

Add Capers and Parsley:
- Stir in the capers and chopped parsley. Let the sauce simmer for 2-3 minutes to reduce slightly.

Finish with Butter:
- Reduce the heat to low, and whisk in the remaining 2 tablespoons of butter until the sauce is smooth and slightly thickened.

Return Chicken to Pan:

- Return the cooked chicken breasts to the skillet, coating them with the lemon butter sauce. Cook for an additional 2-3 minutes to heat through.

Garnish:
- Garnish the Lemon Butter Chicken Piccata with lemon slices.

Serve:
- Serve the chicken over pasta, rice, or with your favorite side dishes. Spoon the lemon butter caper sauce over the chicken.

This Lemon Butter Chicken Piccata is a classic and flavorful dish that combines the richness of butter, the brightness of lemon, and the brininess of capers. It's perfect for a special dinner and pairs well with pasta or rice.

Lemon Butter Chicken Piccata

Ingredients:

- 4 boneless, skinless chicken breasts
- Salt and black pepper, to taste
- 1 cup all-purpose flour, for dredging
- 4 tablespoons unsalted butter, divided
- 2 tablespoons olive oil
- 1/2 cup chicken broth
- 1/2 cup dry white wine
- Juice of 2 lemons
- 1/4 cup capers, drained
- 1/4 cup fresh parsley, chopped
- Lemon slices (for garnish)

Instructions:

Prep Chicken:
- Season the chicken breasts with salt and black pepper.

Dredge in Flour:
- Dredge each chicken breast in flour, shaking off any excess.

Sear Chicken:
- In a large skillet, heat 2 tablespoons of butter and olive oil over medium-high heat. Add the chicken breasts and cook for about 4-5 minutes per side or until golden brown and cooked through. Transfer the cooked chicken to a plate and cover with foil to keep warm.

Make Sauce:
- In the same skillet, add the chicken broth, white wine, and lemon juice. Use a wooden spoon to scrape up any browned bits from the bottom of the pan.

Add Capers and Parsley:
- Stir in the capers and chopped parsley. Let the sauce simmer for 2-3 minutes to reduce slightly.

Finish with Butter:
- Reduce the heat to low, and whisk in the remaining 2 tablespoons of butter until the sauce is smooth and slightly thickened.

Return Chicken to Pan:

- Return the cooked chicken breasts to the skillet, coating them with the lemon butter sauce. Cook for an additional 2-3 minutes to heat through.

Garnish:
- Garnish the Lemon Butter Chicken Piccata with lemon slices.

Serve:
- Serve the chicken over pasta, rice, or with your favorite side dishes. Spoon the lemon butter caper sauce over the chicken.

This Lemon Butter Chicken Piccata is a classic and flavorful dish that combines the richness of butter, the brightness of lemon, and the brininess of capers. It's perfect for a special dinner and pairs well with pasta or rice.

Lemon Coconut Energy Bites

Ingredients:

- 1 cup Medjool dates, pitted
- 1 cup unsweetened shredded coconut
- 1/2 cup raw cashews
- Zest of 2 lemons
- Juice of 1 lemon
- 1 tablespoon chia seeds
- 1/2 teaspoon vanilla extract
- Pinch of salt (optional)
- Additional shredded coconut for rolling (optional)

Instructions:

Prepare Dates:
- If the dates are not soft, soak them in warm water for about 10 minutes. Drain well.

Combine Ingredients:
- In a food processor, combine dates, shredded coconut, raw cashews, lemon zest, lemon juice, chia seeds, vanilla extract, and a pinch of salt if desired.

Process Mixture:
- Process the mixture until it comes together into a sticky, crumbly dough. You should be able to pinch the mixture between your fingers, and it holds together.

Form Energy Bites:
- Take small portions of the mixture and roll them between your palms to form bite-sized energy balls. If the mixture is too sticky, you can wet your hands or dust them with additional shredded coconut.

Optional: Roll in Coconut:
- Optionally, roll the energy bites in additional shredded coconut for a coating.

Chill:
- Place the energy bites in the refrigerator for at least 30 minutes to firm up.

Store:
- Store the Lemon Coconut Energy Bites in an airtight container in the refrigerator for freshness.

Enjoy:
- Enjoy these refreshing and nutritious energy bites as a quick and healthy snack.

These Lemon Coconut Energy Bites are a delightful combination of sweet and tangy flavors, providing a burst of energy and satisfaction. Packed with wholesome ingredients, they make for a convenient and delicious on-the-go snack.

Lemon Basil Shrimp Pasta

Ingredients:

- 8 ounces linguine or your choice of pasta
- 1 pound large shrimp, peeled and deveined
- Salt and black pepper, to taste
- 3 tablespoons olive oil
- 4 cloves garlic, minced
- Zest of 1 lemon
- Juice of 1 lemon
- 1/2 cup cherry tomatoes, halved
- 1/4 cup fresh basil, chopped
- 1/4 cup freshly grated Parmesan cheese (optional)
- Red pepper flakes (optional, for heat)

Instructions:

Cook Pasta:
- Cook the pasta according to package instructions in a large pot of salted boiling water. Drain and set aside.

Season Shrimp:
- Season the shrimp with salt and black pepper.

Sauté Shrimp:
- In a large skillet, heat olive oil over medium-high heat. Add the seasoned shrimp and cook for 2-3 minutes per side or until they turn pink and opaque. Remove the shrimp from the skillet and set aside.

Make Lemon Garlic Sauce:
- In the same skillet, add minced garlic and sauté for about 1 minute until fragrant. Add the lemon zest and lemon juice, stirring to combine.

Combine Pasta and Shrimp:
- Return the cooked pasta to the skillet, tossing it in the lemon garlic sauce. Add the cooked shrimp back to the skillet.

Add Tomatoes and Basil:
- Add halved cherry tomatoes and chopped fresh basil to the pasta and shrimp. Toss everything together until well combined.

Optional: Add Parmesan and Red Pepper Flakes:

- If desired, sprinkle freshly grated Parmesan cheese over the pasta and shrimp. Add red pepper flakes for a bit of heat.

Serve:
- Serve the Lemon Basil Shrimp Pasta warm, garnished with additional fresh basil and a wedge of lemon if desired.

This Lemon Basil Shrimp Pasta is a light and flavorful dish that combines the freshness of lemon and basil with succulent shrimp. It's quick to make and perfect for a satisfying weeknight dinner.

Lemon Herb Quinoa Salad

Ingredients:

For the Quinoa:

- 1 cup quinoa, rinsed
- 2 cups water
- 1/2 teaspoon salt

For the Salad:

- 1 cup cherry tomatoes, halved
- 1 cucumber, diced
- 1/2 red onion, finely chopped
- 1/4 cup fresh parsley, chopped
- 1/4 cup fresh mint, chopped

For the Lemon Herb Dressing:

- 1/4 cup olive oil
- Zest of 1 lemon
- Juice of 1 lemon
- 2 tablespoons fresh basil, chopped
- 1 tablespoon fresh thyme leaves
- 1 clove garlic, minced
- Salt and black pepper, to taste

Instructions:

Prepare Quinoa:

In a medium saucepan, combine the rinsed quinoa, water, and salt. Bring to a boil, then reduce the heat to low, cover, and simmer for 15-20 minutes or until the quinoa is cooked and water is absorbed.
Remove from heat and let it sit, covered, for 5 minutes. Fluff the quinoa with a fork and allow it to cool.

Make Lemon Herb Dressing:

In a small bowl, whisk together olive oil, lemon zest, lemon juice, chopped basil, thyme, minced garlic, salt, and black pepper. Set aside.

Assemble the Salad:

In a large bowl, combine the cooked and cooled quinoa with cherry tomatoes, diced cucumber, chopped red onion, fresh parsley, and fresh mint.
Pour the prepared Lemon Herb Dressing over the quinoa and vegetables. Toss everything together until well combined.
Adjust seasoning with additional salt and pepper, if needed.

Chill and Serve:

Cover the bowl and refrigerate the Lemon Herb Quinoa Salad for at least 1 hour to allow the flavors to meld.
Serve chilled as a refreshing side dish or a light and nutritious main course.

This Lemon Herb Quinoa Salad is a vibrant and flavorful dish that's perfect for a healthy meal or a side dish for gatherings. The combination of fresh herbs and citrusy lemon makes it a refreshing option for any occasion.

Lemon Garlic Butter Grilled Shrimp

Ingredients:

- 1 pound large shrimp, peeled and deveined
- 3 tablespoons unsalted butter, melted
- 3 tablespoons olive oil
- 4 cloves garlic, minced
- Zest of 1 lemon
- Juice of 1 lemon
- 1 teaspoon dried oregano
- 1 teaspoon paprika
- Salt and black pepper, to taste
- Fresh parsley, chopped (for garnish)
- Lemon wedges (for serving)

Instructions:

Prepare Shrimp:
- Pat the shrimp dry with paper towels and place them in a bowl.

Make Marinade:
- In a small bowl, whisk together melted butter, olive oil, minced garlic, lemon zest, lemon juice, dried oregano, paprika, salt, and black pepper.

Marinate Shrimp:
- Pour the marinade over the shrimp and toss to coat them evenly. Allow the shrimp to marinate for about 15-30 minutes.

Preheat Grill:
- Preheat your grill to medium-high heat.

Skewer Shrimp:
- Thread the marinated shrimp onto skewers, ensuring they are well spaced.

Grill Shrimp:
- Place the shrimp skewers on the preheated grill. Grill for 2-3 minutes per side or until the shrimp are opaque and have grill marks.

Baste with Marinade:
- While grilling, baste the shrimp with the remaining marinade for added flavor.

Garnish:

- Once the shrimp are cooked, remove them from the grill. Sprinkle chopped fresh parsley over the grilled shrimp for a burst of color and freshness.

Serve:
- Serve the Lemon Garlic Butter Grilled Shrimp immediately, with lemon wedges on the side for squeezing over the shrimp.

Enjoy these succulent and flavorful Lemon Garlic Butter Grilled Shrimp as a delicious appetizer or as part of a light and refreshing meal. The combination of citrusy lemon, garlic, and butter enhances the natural sweetness of the shrimp, making it a perfect dish for summer grilling.

Lemon Almond Biscotti

Ingredients:

- 2 cups all-purpose flour
- 1 cup granulated sugar
- 1 teaspoon baking powder
- 1/2 teaspoon baking soda
- 1/4 teaspoon salt
- Zest of 2 lemons
- 1/2 cup (1 stick) unsalted butter, softened
- 2 large eggs
- 1 teaspoon vanilla extract
- 1 teaspoon almond extract
- 1 cup whole almonds, toasted and coarsely chopped

For the Lemon Glaze:

- 1 cup powdered sugar
- 2 tablespoons fresh lemon juice
- 1 teaspoon lemon zest

Instructions:

Preheat Oven:
- Preheat your oven to 350°F (175°C). Line a baking sheet with parchment paper.

Toast Almonds:
- Spread the whole almonds on a baking sheet and toast in the preheated oven for about 8-10 minutes or until they are lightly browned. Allow them to cool, then coarsely chop.

Make Dough:
- In a bowl, whisk together the flour, baking powder, baking soda, and salt.

Cream Butter and Sugar:
- In a separate large bowl, cream together the softened butter, granulated sugar, and lemon zest until light and fluffy.

Add Eggs and Extracts:

- Add the eggs one at a time, beating well after each addition. Stir in the vanilla extract and almond extract.

Combine Dry Ingredients:
- Gradually add the dry ingredients to the wet ingredients, mixing just until combined.

Fold in Almonds:
- Gently fold in the toasted and chopped almonds into the dough.

Shape Dough:
- Divide the dough in half. On a floured surface, shape each half into a log about 12 inches long and 2 inches wide. Place the logs on the prepared baking sheet, leaving space between them.

Bake:
- Bake in the preheated oven for 25-30 minutes or until the logs are golden brown and firm to the touch.

Slice Biscotti:
- Remove the logs from the oven and let them cool for about 15 minutes. Reduce the oven temperature to 325°F (160°C). Using a serrated knife, slice the logs diagonally into 1/2-inch thick biscotti.

Bake Again:
- Place the sliced biscotti back on the baking sheet, cut side down. Bake for an additional 15-20 minutes, or until the biscotti are crisp and golden.

Make Lemon Glaze:
- In a small bowl, whisk together the powdered sugar, fresh lemon juice, and lemon zest to make the glaze.

Glaze Biscotti:
- Once the biscotti have cooled, drizzle the lemon glaze over them. Allow the glaze to set before serving.

Serve:
- Enjoy your Lemon Almond Biscotti with a cup of tea or coffee!

These Lemon Almond Biscotti are crunchy, flavorful, and perfect for dipping. The combination of citrusy lemon, toasted almonds, and the sweet glaze makes them a delightful treat for any time of the day.

Lemon Ginger Chicken Stir-Fry

Ingredients:

For the Marinade:

- 1 pound boneless, skinless chicken breasts, thinly sliced
- 2 tablespoons soy sauce
- 1 tablespoon rice vinegar
- 1 tablespoon cornstarch
- 1 teaspoon sesame oil
- 1 teaspoon grated fresh ginger
- 2 cloves garlic, minced

For the Stir-Fry:

- 2 tablespoons vegetable oil
- 1 red bell pepper, thinly sliced
- 1 yellow bell pepper, thinly sliced
- 1 cup snap peas, ends trimmed
- 1 carrot, julienned
- Zest of 1 lemon
- Juice of 1 lemon
- 2 tablespoons soy sauce
- 1 tablespoon honey or maple syrup
- 1 teaspoon grated fresh ginger
- 2 green onions, sliced (for garnish)
- Sesame seeds (for garnish)
- Cooked rice or noodles (for serving)

Instructions:

Marinate the Chicken:

In a bowl, combine sliced chicken with soy sauce, rice vinegar, cornstarch, sesame oil, grated ginger, and minced garlic. Toss to coat the chicken evenly. Let it marinate for at least 15-20 minutes.

Prepare the Stir-Fry:

Heat vegetable oil in a large wok or skillet over medium-high heat.
Add the marinated chicken to the hot wok and stir-fry until the chicken is cooked through and browned. Remove the chicken from the wok and set aside.
In the same wok, add a bit more oil if needed. Add sliced red and yellow bell peppers, snap peas, and julienned carrot. Stir-fry for 2-3 minutes until the vegetables are crisp-tender.
Return the cooked chicken to the wok with the vegetables.
In a small bowl, whisk together lemon zest, lemon juice, soy sauce, honey (or maple syrup), and grated ginger.
Pour the lemon-ginger sauce over the chicken and vegetables. Toss everything together to coat evenly and heat through.
Taste and adjust the seasoning, adding more soy sauce or honey if needed.
Garnish the Lemon Ginger Chicken Stir-Fry with sliced green onions and sesame seeds.
Serve the stir-fry over cooked rice or noodles.

Enjoy this vibrant and zesty Lemon Ginger Chicken Stir-Fry with a perfect balance of flavors. It's a quick and delicious meal that's sure to satisfy your taste buds!

Lemon Basil Vinaigrette

Ingredients:

- 1/4 cup fresh lemon juice
- 1 teaspoon lemon zest
- 2 tablespoons fresh basil, finely chopped
- 1 clove garlic, minced
- 1 tablespoon Dijon mustard
- 1 tablespoon honey
- 1/2 cup extra-virgin olive oil
- Salt and black pepper, to taste

Instructions:

Prepare Ingredients:
- Zest the lemon and squeeze out 1/4 cup of fresh lemon juice. Finely chop the fresh basil and mince the garlic.

Make Vinaigrette:
- In a bowl, whisk together the fresh lemon juice, lemon zest, chopped basil, minced garlic, Dijon mustard, and honey.

Emulsify with Olive Oil:
- While whisking continuously, slowly drizzle in the extra-virgin olive oil to emulsify the vinaigrette. Continue whisking until the dressing is well combined and slightly thickened.

Season:
- Season the Lemon Basil Vinaigrette with salt and black pepper, adjusting the quantities to your taste.

Taste and Adjust:
- Taste the vinaigrette and adjust the flavors if needed. You can add more honey for sweetness or more lemon juice for acidity.

Store:
- Transfer the vinaigrette to a jar or container with a tight-fitting lid. Store it in the refrigerator until ready to use.

Serve:
- Drizzle the Lemon Basil Vinaigrette over your favorite salads, grilled vegetables, or as a marinade for chicken or fish.

This versatile Lemon Basil Vinaigrette adds a burst of fresh and zesty flavor to your dishes. It's a delightful dressing for salads and a fantastic way to enhance the taste of various grilled or roasted ingredients. Shake well before using, and enjoy the bright and herby goodness!

Lemon Herb Couscous

Ingredients:

- 1 cup couscous
- 1 1/4 cups vegetable or chicken broth
- Zest of 1 lemon
- Juice of 1 lemon
- 2 tablespoons fresh parsley, chopped
- 1 tablespoon fresh mint, chopped
- 1 tablespoon fresh chives, chopped
- 2 tablespoons extra-virgin olive oil
- Salt and black pepper, to taste

Instructions:

Prepare Couscous:
- In a saucepan, bring the vegetable or chicken broth to a boil.

Add Couscous:
- Stir in the couscous, cover the saucepan with a lid, and remove it from heat. Let it sit for 5 minutes to allow the couscous to absorb the liquid.

Fluff Couscous:
- After 5 minutes, fluff the couscous with a fork to separate the grains.

Add Lemon Zest and Juice:
- Add the lemon zest and lemon juice to the couscous. Stir gently to incorporate.

Herb Infusion:
- Fold in the chopped parsley, mint, and chives to infuse the couscous with fresh herbal flavors.

Drizzle with Olive Oil:
- Drizzle extra-virgin olive oil over the couscous and toss to coat evenly.

Season:
- Season the Lemon Herb Couscous with salt and black pepper, adjusting to your taste preference.

Serve:
- Serve the Lemon Herb Couscous as a delightful side dish alongside grilled chicken, fish, or vegetables.

This Lemon Herb Couscous is a light and flavorful side dish that pairs well with a variety of main courses. The combination of fresh herbs and citrusy lemon adds a refreshing touch to the couscous, making it a perfect addition to your meals.

Lemon Garlic Butter Shrimp Tacos

Ingredients:

For the Lemon Garlic Butter Shrimp:

- 1 pound large shrimp, peeled and deveined
- Salt and black pepper, to taste
- 3 tablespoons unsalted butter
- 3 cloves garlic, minced
- Zest of 1 lemon
- Juice of 1 lemon
- 1 tablespoon fresh parsley, chopped

For the Tacos:

- 8 small flour or corn tortillas
- Shredded lettuce
- Diced tomatoes
- Sliced avocado
- Sour cream or Greek yogurt (optional)
- Lime wedges (for serving)

Instructions:

Prepare Lemon Garlic Butter Shrimp:

> Season the shrimp with salt and black pepper.
> In a large skillet, melt the butter over medium heat.
> Add minced garlic to the melted butter and sauté for about 1 minute until fragrant.
> Add the shrimp to the skillet and cook for 2-3 minutes per side or until they turn pink and opaque.
> Stir in the lemon zest, lemon juice, and chopped parsley. Cook for an additional minute, making sure the shrimp are well coated in the lemon garlic butter.
> Remove the skillet from heat and set aside.

Assemble Lemon Garlic Butter Shrimp Tacos:

>Warm the tortillas according to package instructions.
>Assemble each taco by placing a portion of the lemon garlic butter shrimp on a tortilla.
>Top the shrimp with shredded lettuce, diced tomatoes, and sliced avocado.
>Optional: Drizzle with sour cream or Greek yogurt for added creaminess.
>Squeeze a lime wedge over the taco for an extra burst of citrus flavor.
>Repeat the process for the remaining tacos.
>Serve the Lemon Garlic Butter Shrimp Tacos immediately.

These Lemon Garlic Butter Shrimp Tacos are a delightful combination of succulent shrimp with zesty lemon and garlic flavors. Customize them with your favorite toppings for a delicious and satisfying meal!

Lemon Raspberry Parfait

Ingredients:

- 1 cup fresh raspberries
- 2 tablespoons granulated sugar
- 1 tablespoon water
- 1 cup Greek yogurt or vanilla yogurt
- Zest of 1 lemon
- 2 tablespoons fresh lemon juice
- 2 tablespoons honey
- 1 cup granola
- Fresh mint leaves (for garnish, optional)

Instructions:

Prepare Raspberry Sauce:

In a small saucepan, combine fresh raspberries, granulated sugar, and water. Cook over medium heat, stirring occasionally, until the raspberries break down and the mixture thickens to a sauce-like consistency. Remove from heat and let it cool.

Prepare Lemon Yogurt:

In a bowl, mix Greek yogurt or vanilla yogurt with lemon zest, fresh lemon juice, and honey. Stir until well combined.

Assemble the Parfait:

In serving glasses or jars, layer the components as follows:
- Start with a spoonful of raspberry sauce at the bottom.
- Add a layer of lemon yogurt.
- Sprinkle granola over the yogurt for added crunch.
- Repeat the layers until you reach the top of the glass, finishing with a drizzle of raspberry sauce.

Top each parfait with fresh raspberries and, if desired, mint leaves for a decorative touch.

Chill the parfaits in the refrigerator for at least 30 minutes before serving.

Serve the Lemon Raspberry Parfait chilled and enjoy the delightful combination of citrusy lemon, sweet raspberry sauce, creamy yogurt, and crunchy granola.

This Lemon Raspberry Parfait is a refreshing and visually appealing dessert that's perfect for a light and elegant treat. The layers of flavors and textures create a delightful balance, making it a great choice for any occasion.

Lemon Herb Chicken Skewers

Ingredients:

For the Marinade:

- 1.5 lbs (about 700g) boneless, skinless chicken breasts, cut into bite-sized pieces
- 3 tablespoons olive oil
- Zest of 1 lemon
- Juice of 1 lemon
- 3 cloves garlic, minced
- 2 tablespoons fresh parsley, chopped
- 1 tablespoon fresh thyme leaves
- 1 teaspoon dried oregano
- Salt and black pepper, to taste

For the Skewers:

- Wooden or metal skewers (if using wooden, soak them in water for 30 minutes before using)
- Cherry tomatoes
- Red onion, cut into chunks
- Bell peppers, cut into chunks

Instructions:

Prepare Marinade:
- In a bowl, whisk together olive oil, lemon zest, lemon juice, minced garlic, chopped parsley, thyme leaves, dried oregano, salt, and black pepper.

Marinate Chicken:
- Place the chicken pieces in a resealable plastic bag or a shallow dish. Pour the marinade over the chicken, ensuring all pieces are well-coated. Seal the bag or cover the dish and refrigerate for at least 30 minutes to marinate. For a deeper flavor, marinate for up to 4 hours.

Preheat Grill or Oven:
- Preheat your grill or oven to medium-high heat.

Assemble Skewers:
- Thread the marinated chicken pieces onto skewers, alternating with cherry tomatoes, red onion chunks, and bell pepper chunks.

Grill or Oven Cook:
- Grill the skewers for about 10-12 minutes, turning occasionally, until the chicken is fully cooked and has a nice char. Alternatively, you can bake them in the oven at 400°F (200°C) for about 15-20 minutes or until done.

Optional: Baste with Marinade:
- Optionally, you can baste the skewers with extra marinade during cooking for added flavor.

Serve:
- Once cooked, remove the Lemon Herb Chicken Skewers from the grill or oven.

Garnish:
- Garnish with additional fresh parsley and lemon wedges.

Serve Hot:
- Serve the skewers hot with your favorite sides, such as rice, couscous, or a fresh salad.

These Lemon Herb Chicken Skewers are bursting with fresh and zesty flavors, making them a perfect addition to your summer grilling menu or a quick and tasty weeknight dinner.

Lemon Butter Artichoke Dip

Ingredients:

- 1 can (14 ounces) artichoke hearts, drained and chopped
- 1 cup grated Parmesan cheese
- 1 cup mayonnaise
- 1 cup shredded mozzarella cheese
- 1/2 cup unsalted butter, softened
- 2 cloves garlic, minced
- Zest of 1 lemon
- Juice of 1 lemon
- 1/4 teaspoon black pepper
- 1/4 teaspoon red pepper flakes (optional, for heat)
- Fresh parsley, chopped (for garnish)

For Serving:

- Sliced baguette, crackers, or vegetable sticks

Instructions:

Preheat Oven:
- Preheat your oven to 375°F (190°C).

Prepare Baking Dish:
- Grease a baking dish (such as a 9x9-inch dish) with butter or cooking spray.

Combine Ingredients:
- In a mixing bowl, combine chopped artichoke hearts, grated Parmesan cheese, mayonnaise, shredded mozzarella cheese, softened butter, minced garlic, lemon zest, lemon juice, black pepper, and red pepper flakes if using. Mix until well combined.

Transfer to Baking Dish:
- Transfer the artichoke mixture to the prepared baking dish, spreading it out evenly.

Bake:
- Bake in the preheated oven for about 25-30 minutes or until the dip is hot and bubbly, and the top is golden brown.

Garnish:

- Remove the Lemon Butter Artichoke Dip from the oven and garnish with chopped fresh parsley.

Serve:
- Serve the dip hot with sliced baguette, crackers, or vegetable sticks for dipping.

Enjoy:
- Enjoy the creamy and flavorful Lemon Butter Artichoke Dip as a delicious appetizer for parties or gatherings.

This Lemon Butter Artichoke Dip combines the richness of butter, the tanginess of lemon, and the savory goodness of artichokes. It's a crowd-pleasing appetizer that's perfect for entertaining or as a comforting treat for yourself.

Lemon Basil Pesto Hummus

Ingredients:

- 1 can (15 ounces) chickpeas, drained and rinsed
- 1/4 cup fresh basil leaves, packed
- 1/4 cup grated Parmesan cheese
- 3 tablespoons pine nuts
- 2 tablespoons fresh lemon juice
- 2 tablespoons extra-virgin olive oil
- 2 tablespoons tahini
- 2 cloves garlic, minced
- Zest of 1 lemon
- Salt and black pepper, to taste
- Water (as needed for desired consistency)

Instructions:

Prepare Ingredients:
- Drain and rinse the chickpeas. Zest the lemon and squeeze out fresh lemon juice.

Make Basil Pesto:
- In a food processor, combine fresh basil leaves, grated Parmesan cheese, pine nuts, garlic, and half of the lemon zest. Pulse until ingredients are finely chopped.

Add Chickpeas:
- Add the drained chickpeas to the food processor.

Blend:
- Blend the ingredients while slowly adding fresh lemon juice, olive oil, tahini, and the remaining lemon zest. Continue blending until smooth.

Adjust Consistency:
- If the hummus is too thick, add water, one tablespoon at a time, until you reach your desired consistency.

Season:
- Season the Lemon Basil Pesto Hummus with salt and black pepper to taste. Blend again to incorporate the seasoning.

Taste and Adjust:
- Taste the hummus and adjust the lemon, salt, or other ingredients as needed to suit your preferences.

Serve:
- Transfer the Lemon Basil Pesto Hummus to a serving bowl. Drizzle with a bit of extra olive oil and garnish with additional pine nuts or fresh basil leaves.

Enjoy:
- Serve the hummus with pita bread, tortilla chips, vegetable sticks, or as a flavorful spread.

This Lemon Basil Pesto Hummus is a delightful twist on traditional hummus, combining the freshness of basil and lemon with the nuttiness of pine nuts. It makes for a vibrant and flavorful dip that's perfect for parties, snacks, or a light appetizer.

Lemon Garlic Butter Green Beans

Ingredients:

- 1 pound fresh green beans, trimmed
- 2 tablespoons unsalted butter
- 2 tablespoons olive oil
- 3 cloves garlic, minced
- Zest of 1 lemon
- Juice of 1 lemon
- Salt and black pepper, to taste
- Lemon slices (for garnish, optional)
- Fresh parsley, chopped (for garnish, optional)

Instructions:

Blanch Green Beans:
- Bring a large pot of salted water to a boil. Add the trimmed green beans and blanch them for 2-3 minutes until they are bright green and slightly tender but still crisp. Immediately transfer the green beans to a bowl of ice water to stop the cooking process. Drain and set aside.

Sauté Garlic:
- In a large skillet, heat olive oil and butter over medium heat. Add minced garlic and sauté for 1-2 minutes until fragrant.

Add Green Beans:
- Add the blanched green beans to the skillet. Toss them in the garlic-infused oil and butter to coat evenly.

Lemon Infusion:
- Zest the lemon directly into the skillet and squeeze the lemon juice over the green beans. Toss to combine, allowing the lemon flavors to infuse into the green beans.

Season:
- Season the green beans with salt and black pepper, adjusting to your taste preference. Continue to toss until the green beans are well-coated.

Finish Cooking:
- Cook the green beans for an additional 2-3 minutes until they are fully heated through and have absorbed the flavors.

Garnish:

- Optionally, garnish the Lemon Garlic Butter Green Beans with lemon slices and chopped fresh parsley for a burst of color and freshness.

Serve:
- Transfer the green beans to a serving platter and serve immediately.

These Lemon Garlic Butter Green Beans are a vibrant and flavorful side dish that complements a variety of meals. The combination of citrusy lemon, aromatic garlic, and rich butter enhances the natural freshness of the green beans. Enjoy them as a delicious and nutritious addition to your dinner table.

Lemon Berry Smoothie

Ingredients:

- 1 cup mixed berries (strawberries, blueberries, raspberries)
- 1 ripe banana, peeled
- 1/2 cup Greek yogurt (or yogurt of choice)
- 1/2 cup almond milk (or milk of choice)
- 1 tablespoon honey (optional, for sweetness)
- Juice of 1 lemon
- Ice cubes (optional)

Instructions:

Prepare Ingredients:
- Wash the berries and hull the strawberries if needed. Peel the ripe banana.

Blend Smoothie:
- In a blender, combine the mixed berries, banana, Greek yogurt, almond milk, honey (if using), and the juice of one lemon.

Blend Until Smooth:
- Blend the ingredients until smooth and creamy. If you prefer a thicker smoothie, you can add ice cubes and blend again until well incorporated.

Taste and Adjust:
- Taste the smoothie and adjust the sweetness by adding more honey if needed. You can also adjust the consistency by adding more almond milk or ice cubes.

Blend Again (Optional):
- If you added additional ingredients, blend again until everything is well mixed.

Serve:
- Pour the Lemon Berry Smoothie into glasses and serve immediately.

Garnish (Optional):
- Optionally, garnish the smoothie with a slice of lemon or a few whole berries for a decorative touch.

Enjoy:
- Enjoy this refreshing and nutritious Lemon Berry Smoothie as a quick and delicious breakfast, snack, or post-workout drink.

Feel free to customize this smoothie by adding other fruits, greens, or seeds to suit your taste preferences and nutritional needs. The combination of berries and lemon provides a delightful burst of flavors, making this smoothie a perfect way to start your day.

Lemon Sage Roasted Chicken

Ingredients:

- 1 whole chicken (about 4-5 pounds)
- Salt and black pepper, to taste
- 2 lemons, sliced
- Fresh sage leaves
- 4 cloves garlic, minced
- 1/4 cup olive oil
- 2 tablespoons fresh lemon juice
- Zest of 1 lemon
- 1 tablespoon Dijon mustard
- 1 teaspoon dried sage
- 1 teaspoon paprika

Instructions:

Preheat Oven:
- Preheat your oven to 425°F (220°C).

Prepare Chicken:
- Pat the whole chicken dry with paper towels. Season the chicken inside and out with salt and black pepper.

Create Flavor Mixture:
- In a bowl, combine minced garlic, olive oil, fresh lemon juice, lemon zest, Dijon mustard, dried sage, and paprika. Mix well to create a flavor mixture.

Lift Skin and Rub Mixture:
- Carefully lift the skin of the chicken and rub about half of the flavor mixture underneath the skin, spreading it evenly over the breasts and thighs.

Coat Exterior:
- Rub the remaining mixture over the outside of the chicken, ensuring it is well-coated.

Stuff with Lemons and Sage:
- Place sliced lemons and fresh sage leaves inside the cavity of the chicken.

Truss Chicken (Optional):
- If desired, truss the chicken using kitchen twine to help it cook more evenly.

Roast in Oven:
- Place the chicken in a roasting pan or on a wire rack set in a baking sheet. Roast in the preheated oven for about 15 minutes.

Reduce Heat and Continue Roasting:
- After 15 minutes, reduce the oven temperature to 375°F (190°C) and continue roasting for approximately 1 to 1.5 hours, or until the internal temperature reaches 165°F (74°C) in the thickest part of the thigh.

Baste Occasionally:
- Baste the chicken with pan juices every 20-30 minutes to keep it moist and flavorful.

Rest Before Carving:
- Once the chicken is cooked, remove it from the oven and let it rest for 15-20 minutes before carving.

Carve and Serve:
- Carve the Lemon Sage Roasted Chicken, garnish with additional fresh sage if desired, and serve with the roasted lemons.

This Lemon Sage Roasted Chicken is infused with citrusy and herby flavors, making it a delicious and comforting dish. It's perfect for a family dinner or a special occasion.

Enjoy the succulent and aromatic roast with your favorite side dishes.

Lemon Herb Quiche

Ingredients:

For the Quiche Filling:

- 1 pre-made pie crust (or homemade, if preferred)
- 4 large eggs
- 1 cup whole milk
- 1 cup heavy cream
- Zest of 1 lemon
- 2 tablespoons fresh lemon juice
- 1 tablespoon fresh parsley, finely chopped
- 1 tablespoon fresh chives, finely chopped
- 1 tablespoon fresh dill, finely chopped
- Salt and black pepper, to taste
- 1 cup shredded Gruyere or Swiss cheese

For Garnish:

- Additional fresh herbs for garnish

Instructions:

Preheat Oven:
- Preheat your oven to 375°F (190°C).

Prepare Pie Crust:
- If using a pre-made pie crust, follow the package instructions for pre-baking. If using homemade crust, blind bake it by lining the crust with parchment paper and filling it with pie weights or dried beans. Bake for about 15 minutes, then remove the weights and parchment and bake for an additional 5 minutes until lightly golden.

Prepare Filling:
- In a bowl, whisk together eggs, whole milk, heavy cream, lemon zest, lemon juice, chopped parsley, chopped chives, chopped dill, salt, and black pepper.

Add Cheese:
- Stir in the shredded Gruyere or Swiss cheese into the egg mixture.

Assemble and Bake:

- Pour the egg and herb mixture into the pre-baked pie crust.

Bake:
- Bake in the preheated oven for 35-40 minutes or until the quiche is set and the top is golden brown. If the crust edges are browning too quickly, cover them with foil.

Cool and Garnish:
- Allow the Lemon Herb Quiche to cool for at least 15-20 minutes before slicing. Garnish with additional fresh herbs.

Serve:
- Serve the quiche slices warm or at room temperature.

This Lemon Herb Quiche is a delightful combination of citrusy lemon and fresh herbs, creating a light and flavorful dish. It's perfect for brunch, lunch, or a light dinner. Enjoy it with a side salad for a complete and satisfying meal.

Lemon Butter Caper Pasta

Ingredients:

- 8 ounces (about 225g) linguine or your favorite pasta
- 2 tablespoons unsalted butter
- 2 tablespoons olive oil
- 3 cloves garlic, minced
- 2 tablespoons capers, drained
- Zest of 1 lemon
- Juice of 1 lemon
- Salt and black pepper, to taste
- Red pepper flakes (optional, for heat)
- Fresh parsley, chopped (for garnish)
- Grated Parmesan cheese (for serving)

Instructions:

Cook Pasta:
- Cook the pasta according to the package instructions in a large pot of salted boiling water until al dente. Drain and set aside.

Prepare Lemon Butter Caper Sauce:
- In a large skillet, heat the butter and olive oil over medium heat. Add the minced garlic and sauté for 1-2 minutes until fragrant.

Add Capers:
- Stir in the capers and continue to sauté for another minute.

Add Lemon Zest and Juice:
- Add the lemon zest and lemon juice to the skillet. Stir to combine.

Season:
- Season the sauce with salt and black pepper to taste. If you like a bit of heat, you can also add red pepper flakes.

Combine with Pasta:
- Add the cooked and drained pasta to the skillet. Toss the pasta in the lemon butter caper sauce until well coated.

Garnish:
- Garnish the Lemon Butter Caper Pasta with chopped fresh parsley.

Serve:

- Serve the pasta immediately, and if desired, top with grated Parmesan cheese.

This Lemon Butter Caper Pasta is a quick and flavorful dish that combines the brightness of lemon with the savory richness of butter and the briny pop of capers. It's a simple yet elegant pasta dish that can be enjoyed on its own or paired with your favorite protein.

Lemon Rosemary Focaccia

Ingredients:

For the Focaccia Dough:

- 4 cups all-purpose flour
- 1 1/2 cups warm water (110°F/43°C)
- 2 teaspoons active dry yeast
- 1 teaspoon sugar
- 1/4 cup olive oil
- 1 teaspoon salt

For Topping:

- Zest of 2 lemons
- 2 tablespoons fresh rosemary, chopped
- 1/4 cup olive oil
- Coarse sea salt, for sprinkling

Instructions:

Prepare Focaccia Dough:

  Activate Yeast:
  - In a bowl, combine warm water, active dry yeast, and sugar. Let it sit for 5-10 minutes until it becomes frothy.

  Combine Ingredients:
  - In a large mixing bowl, combine the flour and salt. Add the frothy yeast mixture and olive oil. Mix until a dough forms.

  Knead Dough:
  - Transfer the dough to a floured surface and knead for about 8-10 minutes until it becomes smooth and elastic. Alternatively, you can use a stand mixer with a dough hook.

  First Rise:
  - Place the dough in a lightly oiled bowl, cover it with a damp cloth, and let it rise in a warm place for 1-2 hours or until it doubles in size.

Shape and Second Rise:

Preheat Oven:
- Preheat your oven to 425°F (220°C).

Prepare Baking Pan:
- Grease a baking pan or line it with parchment paper. Drizzle some olive oil on the pan.

Shape Dough:
- Transfer the risen dough to the prepared baking pan. Gently stretch and press the dough to cover the pan evenly.

Second Rise:
- Cover the pan with a damp cloth and let the dough rise for an additional 30-45 minutes.

Topping and Baking:

Make Indentations:
- Use your fingers to make indentations all over the surface of the dough.

Drizzle Olive Oil:
- Drizzle olive oil over the top of the dough, making sure it goes into the indentations.

Sprinkle Lemon Zest and Rosemary:
- Sprinkle the lemon zest and chopped rosemary evenly over the dough.

Sprinkle Sea Salt:
- Sprinkle coarse sea salt over the top for added flavor.

Bake:
- Bake in the preheated oven for 20-25 minutes or until the focaccia is golden brown and sounds hollow when tapped on the bottom.

Cool and Serve:
- Allow the Lemon Rosemary Focaccia to cool slightly before slicing. Serve warm and enjoy!

This Lemon Rosemary Focaccia is a delightful and aromatic bread that makes a great accompaniment to meals or a tasty snack on its own. The combination of citrusy lemon, fragrant rosemary, and the olive oil-infused crust creates a flavorful and satisfying treat.

Lemon Garlic Butter Artichokes

Ingredients:

- 2 large artichokes
- 1 lemon, sliced
- 4 cloves garlic, minced
- 1/2 cup unsalted butter
- 2 tablespoons olive oil
- Salt and black pepper, to taste
- Fresh parsley, chopped (for garnish, optional)

Instructions:

Prepare Artichokes:
- Trim the stem of each artichoke, leaving about an inch. Cut off the top 1/3 of each artichoke, and trim the pointed tips of the remaining leaves. Use kitchen scissors to trim any sharp edges.

Steam Artichokes:
- Fill a large pot with about 2 inches of water. Place a steamer basket inside and add the sliced lemon to the water. Bring it to a simmer.

Steam Artichokes:
- Place the prepared artichokes in the steamer basket, facing upward. Cover the pot with a lid and steam for 30-45 minutes, or until the outer leaves can be easily pulled off.

Prepare Garlic Butter Sauce:
- In a small saucepan, melt the butter and olive oil over medium heat. Add minced garlic and sauté for 1-2 minutes until fragrant. Remove from heat.

Season:
- Season the garlic butter sauce with salt and black pepper to taste.

Preheat Grill (Optional):
- If you prefer to finish the artichokes on the grill for a smoky flavor, preheat your grill to medium-high.

Brush with Garlic Butter:
- Using a brush or spoon, generously brush the artichokes with the garlic butter sauce, making sure to get the mixture between the leaves.

Grill (Optional):

- If using a grill, place the garlic butter-coated artichokes on the preheated grill for about 5-10 minutes, turning occasionally, until they develop a nice char.

Garnish and Serve:
- Transfer the artichokes to a serving platter. Garnish with chopped fresh parsley if desired. Serve with additional garlic butter on the side for dipping.

Enjoy:
- To eat, pull off the leaves, dip them in the garlic butter, and scrape the tender part with your teeth. Continue until you reach the heart, which can be cut into pieces and enjoyed with the remaining garlic butter.

These Lemon Garlic Butter Artichokes are a delicious and elegant appetizer or side dish. The combination of steaming and grilling imparts a delightful flavor, while the garlic butter adds richness and depth. Enjoy this flavorful and satisfying dish with friends or as a special treat for yourself.

Lemon Basil Risotto

Ingredients:

- 1 1/2 cups Arborio rice
- 4 cups vegetable or chicken broth, kept warm
- 1 cup dry white wine
- 1/2 cup grated Parmesan cheese
- 1/4 cup unsalted butter
- 1/4 cup olive oil
- 1 small onion, finely chopped
- 2 cloves garlic, minced
- Zest of 1 lemon
- Juice of 1 lemon
- 1/4 cup fresh basil, chopped
- Salt and black pepper, to taste

Instructions:

Prepare Broth:
- Heat the vegetable or chicken broth in a saucepan and keep it warm over low heat.

Sauté Onion and Garlic:
- In a large, heavy-bottomed pot, heat olive oil and 2 tablespoons of butter over medium heat. Add finely chopped onion and cook until translucent. Add minced garlic and sauté for another 1-2 minutes until fragrant.

Toast Rice:
- Add Arborio rice to the pot and stir to coat the rice with the oil, onions, and garlic. Toast the rice for 1-2 minutes until it becomes slightly translucent around the edges.

Deglaze with Wine:
- Pour in the dry white wine, stirring continuously, until the wine is mostly absorbed by the rice.

Add Broth:
- Begin adding the warm broth, one ladle at a time, to the rice. Stir continuously and allow the liquid to be mostly absorbed before adding the next ladle of broth. Continue this process until the rice is creamy and cooked to al dente texture.

Finish with Lemon and Basil:
- Once the rice is cooked, stir in the remaining butter, grated Parmesan cheese, lemon zest, lemon juice, and chopped fresh basil. Season with salt and black pepper to taste.

Adjust Consistency:
- If needed, add more warm broth or hot water to achieve the desired creamy consistency.

Serve:
- Serve the Lemon Basil Risotto immediately, garnished with extra Parmesan cheese and fresh basil if desired.

Enjoy:
- Enjoy this vibrant and flavorful Lemon Basil Risotto as a delicious side dish or a satisfying main course.

This Lemon Basil Risotto is a delightful dish with the bright flavors of lemon and basil enhancing the creamy richness of the risotto. It's perfect for a special dinner or whenever you crave a comforting and elegant meal.

Lemon Butter Garlic Shrimp Skewers

Ingredients:

- 1 pound large shrimp, peeled and deveined
- 1/4 cup unsalted butter, melted
- 3 cloves garlic, minced
- Zest of 1 lemon
- Juice of 1 lemon
- 2 tablespoons fresh parsley, chopped
- Salt and black pepper, to taste
- Wooden or metal skewers, soaked in water if using wooden

Instructions:

Prepare Shrimp:
- If using wooden skewers, soak them in water for at least 30 minutes to prevent burning during grilling.

Marinate Shrimp:
- In a bowl, combine melted butter, minced garlic, lemon zest, lemon juice, chopped parsley, salt, and black pepper. Mix well to create the marinade.

Thread Shrimp onto Skewers:
- Thread the peeled and deveined shrimp onto the skewers, ensuring they are evenly distributed.

Brush with Marinade:
- Brush the shrimp skewers with the prepared lemon butter garlic marinade, making sure to coat them thoroughly.

Preheat Grill or Grill Pan:
- Preheat your grill or grill pan over medium-high heat.

Grill Shrimp:
- Place the shrimp skewers on the preheated grill. Grill for 2-3 minutes per side, or until the shrimp are opaque and have grill marks.

Baste with Marinade:
- While grilling, baste the shrimp with additional marinade to keep them moist and flavorful.

Garnish:
- Once the shrimp are cooked, remove them from the grill. Garnish with additional chopped parsley.

Serve:
- Serve the Lemon Butter Garlic Shrimp Skewers hot, either as an appetizer or as part of a meal.

Enjoy:
- Enjoy these succulent and flavorful shrimp skewers with a side of rice, salad, or your favorite dipping sauce.

These Lemon Butter Garlic Shrimp Skewers are a quick and delicious dish that's perfect for a summer barbecue or a light and flavorful meal. The combination of zesty lemon, garlic, and butter creates a mouthwatering marinade that enhances the natural sweetness of the shrimp.

Lemon Thyme Roasted Vegetables

Ingredients:

- 4 cups mixed vegetables, such as carrots, potatoes, zucchini, bell peppers, and red onions, cut into bite-sized pieces
- 2 tablespoons olive oil
- Zest of 1 lemon
- Juice of 1 lemon
- 2 tablespoons fresh thyme leaves
- 3 cloves garlic, minced
- Salt and black pepper, to taste

Instructions:

Preheat Oven:
- Preheat your oven to 400°F (200°C).

Prepare Vegetables:
- Wash, peel, and chop the vegetables into bite-sized pieces. For a variety of textures, you can include root vegetables like carrots and potatoes, as well as softer vegetables like zucchini and bell peppers.

Make Lemon Thyme Marinade:
- In a bowl, combine olive oil, lemon zest, lemon juice, fresh thyme leaves, minced garlic, salt, and black pepper. Mix well to create the marinade.

Coat Vegetables:
- Place the chopped vegetables in a large mixing bowl. Pour the lemon thyme marinade over the vegetables and toss until they are evenly coated.

Roast Vegetables:
- Spread the coated vegetables in a single layer on a baking sheet lined with parchment paper.

Roast in the Oven:
- Roast in the preheated oven for 30-35 minutes, or until the vegetables are tender and have developed a golden brown color. Stir the vegetables halfway through the roasting time to ensure even cooking.

Garnish (Optional):
- Garnish the Lemon Thyme Roasted Vegetables with additional fresh thyme leaves before serving, if desired.

Serve:

- Serve the roasted vegetables as a flavorful and vibrant side dish to complement your main course.

Enjoy:
- Enjoy the bright and herby flavors of these Lemon Thyme Roasted Vegetables as a delicious addition to your meals.

This dish is not only visually appealing with its colorful assortment of vegetables but also bursts with the fresh and zesty combination of lemon and thyme. It's a versatile side dish that pairs well with various proteins or can be enjoyed on its own.

Lemon Cilantro Grilled Chicken

Ingredients:

- 4 boneless, skinless chicken breasts
- 1/4 cup olive oil
- Zest of 1 lemon
- Juice of 2 lemons
- 3 cloves garlic, minced
- 1/4 cup fresh cilantro, chopped
- 1 teaspoon ground cumin
- 1 teaspoon paprika
- Salt and black pepper, to taste
- Lemon wedges and fresh cilantro for garnish

Instructions:

Prepare Marinade:
- In a bowl, whisk together olive oil, lemon zest, lemon juice, minced garlic, chopped cilantro, ground cumin, paprika, salt, and black pepper. This mixture will serve as the marinade for the chicken.

Marinate Chicken:
- Place the chicken breasts in a large resealable plastic bag or shallow dish. Pour the marinade over the chicken, making sure each piece is well-coated. Seal the bag or cover the dish and refrigerate for at least 30 minutes, or preferably 2-4 hours to allow the flavors to infuse.

Preheat Grill:
- Preheat your grill to medium-high heat.

Grill Chicken:
- Remove the chicken from the marinade and discard the marinade. Grill the chicken breasts for about 6-8 minutes per side or until they reach an internal temperature of 165°F (74°C) and are cooked through. The exact cooking time may vary depending on the thickness of the chicken breasts.

Rest and Garnish:
- Allow the grilled chicken to rest for a few minutes before slicing. Garnish with fresh cilantro and lemon wedges.

Serve:

- Serve the Lemon Cilantro Grilled Chicken with your favorite side dishes, such as rice, salad, or grilled vegetables.

Enjoy:
- Enjoy the flavorful and zesty combination of lemon and cilantro in this grilled chicken dish. It's perfect for a light and refreshing meal, especially during the warmer seasons.

This Lemon Cilantro Grilled Chicken is a simple and delicious recipe that brings out the natural flavors of the chicken while infusing it with the bright and herbaceous notes of lemon and cilantro. It's a great option for a quick and tasty grilled dinner.

www.ingramcontent.com/pod-product-compliance
Lightning Source LLC
LaVergne TN
LVHW061938070526
838199LV00060B/3871